BELONG

GUSTAVO CROCKER

JERRY KESTER

STEPHANIE LOBDELL

BELONG

RETRACING
THE WAY OF
GOD'S
EMBRACING
LOVE

𝒇

THE FOUNDRY
PUBLISHING®

Copyright © 2021 by The Foundry Publishing
The Foundry Publishing®
PO Box 419527
Kansas City, MO 64141
thefoundrypublishing.com

978-0-8341-4033-2

Printed in the
United States of America

Cover Design: Brandon Hill
Interior Design: Sharon Page

Library of Congress Cataloging-in-Publication Data

A complete catalog record for this book is available from the Library of Congress.

10 9 8 7 6 5 4 3 2 1

CONTENTS

INTRODUCTION
Gustavo Crocker

It was October 2017, and I had been invited by Jerry Kester to travel to Seattle, Washington, and meet with his leadership team to dream about a new model for effectively communicating the message of Christ in such a diverse, post-Christian city in the United States. The day before I met with the team of church planters, I decided to walk through the city and visit some of the cultural and social centers that had taken over what used to be the Christian centers. My walk reminded me of my years as a director of missionary work in Eurasia, and the times when I had met local leaders with similar dreams in cities like London, Manchester, Frankfurt, and Rotterdam, to name a few.

In the course of our meeting the following day, I shared with the team some of the lessons we had learned with the church in Europe about the need to shift the Bs in our evangelism models (believing, behaving, becoming, and belonging) that had placed belonging at the very end—a mistaken practice that almost alienated millions of city dwellers who didn't find the need for faith, fellowship, and a church in their lives, particularly under the circumstances in which church had been presented to them.

After the presentation of these lessons and the new paradigm, Jerry asked me if I could present the teachings to his assembly—the annual gathering of clergy and lay leaders from the Washington Pacific region of the United States. Though his request was unusual, I accepted the invitation and presented what became the philosophical construct for this book. Much to my surprise, many pastors and lay leaders from that gathering asked for further conversation on the subject, so Jerry and I started thinking about putting those thoughts together in the form of a book that would help pastors and leaders embrace what many of them were and are already doing in reorienting the church to accomplish the mission of God for their generation.

As Jerry and I thought about this project, we agreed that the format of the book needed to help us deliver the content in a way that readers would identify with it. Because we hope to mobilize young pastors for effective ministry in their contexts, I thought of a format I liked from a book written by millennials to impact millennials and the church at large. *Routes and Radishes*[1] was written in conversational dialogue by five young authors who wanted to share their

1. Mark Russell, Allen Yeh, Michelle Sanchez, Chelle Stearns, and Dwight Friesen, *Routes and Radishes: And Other Things to Talk*

views about evangelicalism while allowing space for the expression of one another's opinions as a way to start a broader conversation among their readers.

This is the format that we chose for this book. Originally, the idea was to invite someone to review our musings and serve as a moderator of our dialogue. However, as the project took shape, we wanted to include in the writing team a millennial author who understood the church, who was willing to express her opinions and challenge ours, and who could help us understand an audience we have mainly understood through reading and interaction. Stephanie Lobdell joined the project and quickly became a key thought partner in this book.

As you read, we hope you will identify with at least one of us in your journey to be part of the church that Christ commissioned to fulfill God's mission. Above all, we hope you will be able to find ways for your ministry to be enriched by reorienting the church in the way Christ intended for it to be.

---

about at the Evangelical Crossroads (Grand Rapids: Zondervan, 2010).

1. WE BELONG, WE BELIEVE
Growing Up as Church People

Jerry's Story

For all but one of my six and a half decades of life I've lived in the U.S. Northwest. I had extended stays in Oklahoma and Kansas, where I picked up a couple of degrees and a wife and son, but I was just visiting. I am a Northwesterner by heritage, birth, and choice. My view of life is shaped in ways that I'm not likely aware of by the culture of the Northwest. I was born in Oregon, not far from where my father grew up, on land that was homesteaded by his grandfather. All my early education happened in the Treasure Valley of Idaho. When I'm asked where I'm from, I say Boise, Idaho. Having lived for a time in the Bible Belt while I was in school, I know that my experience is significantly different from that of my Southern college classmates. The kind of influence that the church wielded in Oklahoma City in all aspects of life in the 1970s was a surprise to me as an outsider.

It's not that my friends in Boise weren't religious—it was just something more privately held and less culturally dominant. When I flip the pages of the yearbook in my mind and think about my friends, I see that they were all connected to one church or another. Even if their families rarely attended, I can't think of many who would have been considered nonreligious. The options for religious expression all fell within the broadest definition of Christianity, somewhere on the spectrum from Catholic to Mormon. Not everyone was connected to some visible expression of faith, but generally people believed that they should be. Most thought the quality of the lives and families of people who had faith and practiced it was better than those who didn't. If someone ran for public office, listing a religious affiliation was important. I did not know an atheist in southern Idaho when I was growing up.

Just as the religious landscape in my hometown of Boise was not the same as the religious landscape in Oklahoma City, neither was it the same in Seattle, Washington. It has always been true that the farther north and west you go in the U.S., the less influence the church has had in the shaping of culture.

Western Washington—where I oversee the ministry of local congregations in the Church of the Nazarene—has always been one of the places where the church has had less influence. This trend toward privately held religious views has continued to intensify into indifference, even hostility, toward the notion of God and toward traditional practices of worship.

Agnosticism and skepticism are proudly held virtues in Seattle. Where I live, nonreligious people often see themselves as morally superior to religious people in general, and to Christians specifically.

It has been widely reported that people who claim no religion are a rapidly growing segment of society. In the Northwest, those who check the box for "none" in answer to questions related to religious preference are the fastest-growing demographic, especially among young people. Church culture that once held a central and privileged place in society has been pushed to the margins and is often viewed as irrelevant, at best and dangerous or hateful, at worst. I am old enough to remember when the public-school day started with Scripture and prayer; those days are certainly a distant memory.

It would be nice to think that those who've grown up in homes where the church played an important, if not central, role in the identity of the family would be immune to this secular shift, but recent studies from social research institutions and observations of local church ministries reveal just the opposite. It is a simple truth that, if the church in its current structure is to have a future, there will have to be a reversal of this trend. Because the church and its existence did not originate with us, we want to be cautious about assuming we can control its future, but we have been left with a sacred trust, and we are obligated to faithfully steward what we have inherited. God supplies seed, sun, water, and soil, but we are still responsible for planting and weeding the garden.

Gustavo's Story

I was born and raised in Guatemala, where I grew up attending the church where my parents were saved through the ministry of missionaries. When I first came to the United States in 1992, I was a young architect visiting as a Fulbright Scholar, and I needed to learn the language and the culture before going to graduate school, so the Fulbright Commission sent me to learn English in Carbondale, Illinois. My first exposure to American culture was as a Guatemalan college professor living in a dorm for college freshmen and sophomores. Everybody looked bigger than me. Everyone ate a lot more than me. I had to learn English—they sent me to a live in a college dorm in full immersion for that very purpose. The goal was to learn English in eight months—from zero to grad school in eight months! So I had to talk in English, I had to listen in English, I had to watch TV in English —everything in English.

It was 1992, and they had told me that the best way to learn the language was to watch a combination of news, sports, and sitcoms. That combination would put me in contact with the culture, which is how I came across the theme song for the sitcom *Cheers*, a top show in the U.S. at the time. As I listened attentively to the song, I got to thinking, *Wow. That's the best slogan for church!* If you just listen to the words, you may come to agree with me because "sometimes you want to go where everybody knows your name. Where our troubles are all the same. Sometimes you want to go where everyone knows your name."

That introduction to American culture provided more than an intriguing observation on church and culture. It also prepared me to watch the church in its various expressions in the United States and, later, Europe. It allowed me to see that a lot of what we define as the norms and mores of church sometimes have a lot of culture and society and very little of Scripture and theology. I arrived in the States as a layperson with the cultural baggage of my beloved denomination that, more often than not, was better known by its organizational structure, its *Manual*, and its governance than by its doctrine. I had been shaped by the combination of scriptural truths learned from my childhood and by the cultural norms imposed upon the life of the church through the interpretations of our polity.

There were many things that, growing up in Guatemala, had been ingrained as fundamentals of the church to which I belonged. To my surprise, some of these fundamentals were not an issue for the same denominational family in the United States—the same family that had sent the missionaries decades earlier to share the doctrine and the values of the church they were developing. We were given norms with regard to our relationship with Catholics, our relationship with music, with sports—you name it. Surprisingly, when I arrived in America, none of these norms were, well, *norms* in the average congregation in America, even though we shared the same essentials of doctrine, polity, and the global connection.

Years later, I found myself serving in Europe at the center of postmodernism and post-Christendom. While serving the church in Europe, I realized that there were many cultural norms that were impacted by the philosophical development of European society in the twentieth century, which made the European church look, worship, and gather differently than the American church, and significantly differently than my native Guatemalan church.

This diverse understanding of what constitutes the community of believers within a tightly developed theological and ecclesiological framework made me think that sometimes we allow our cultural interpretations of community to take over the biblical interpretation of the kingdom of God and its application to Christ's church. In other words, in our efforts to maintain the orthodoxy of the faith (which is absolutely essential and necessary), we have allowed our cultural biases to determine who belongs to the fellowship of followers while equating such fellowship to our own agreed-upon definition of community.

The confusion between what constitutes the fellowship of the followers and the church community of agreed-upon shared values is what led me to think about reorientation. One of the legacies of modernism has been the overemphasis on systems and linear processes, and the church has not escaped this emphasis. We have focused on the community of agreed-upon values as the measure for belonging in the church. We have led people to think that they belong in the church only once they have met all the criteria that our community has agreed upon for welcoming those who have become part of our family. In other words, we have told people that they *belong* only once they have *become* part of the community—which makes the kingdom of God rather exclusionary.

Stephanie's Story

In December of 1941 my great-grandfather Robert (Bob) Miller left the red dirt of Oklahoma for the salty Pacific air of Bremerton, Washington, to work in the Navy shipyards. After much cajoling from a persistent coworker, Bob and his wife, Erma, herded their three daughters into a pew at Bremerton Church of the Nazarene, determined to silence his enthusiastic friend by showing up for church just this once. At the end of the service, all five members of the Miller family knelt at the altar to surrender their lives to Jesus.

Hundreds of miles away, in the snow country of Minnesota, another family made their way to the local Nazarene church. Snow towered on both sides of the street, but inclement weather was no reason to miss worship. My great-grandparents Harlo and Frances Angier bundled their children against the subzero temperatures and directed their feet to the sanctuary.

Thus begins the faith story of my family. It is a story of unwavering faithfulness of laypeople giving their lives to the church for the sake of the kingdom of God. It comes as no surprise that my parents, bearing witness to that heritage of faithfulness, answered the call to vocational ministry—and so too me.

I have no experience of being an outsider to the faith, or of feeling out of place at church. As the child of a pastor, the church felt like it belonged to me. It was a second home where I felt very much at ease. I flitted through the building, greeting and embracing a dozen people before I settled in my Sunday school classroom each week. I knew myself to be loved by God, and, although I could not articulate it as a child, I was aware of and responsive to the divine invitation to be part of God's work in the world.

I left home to attend a denominational college, eager to begin my academic preparation to serve the church. Once again, I felt at home. The way of life, the values, even the code of conduct, felt familiar and natural. My egocentrism and nascent critical-thinking skills allowed me to float through my first year under the impression that my experience was everyone's experience.

Late in the spring of my freshman year, I joined a gaggle of my dorm mates and headed to the gym to attend the annual talent show. It was a classic compilation of skits, cringey musical performances, and awkward standup. As the show neared the end, a young man walked onstage. I recognized him as a student athlete but knew nothing about him other than the fact that he seemed to move in what I perceived to be a questionable, fringe crowd. He was visibly nervous. Sweat glistened on his face as he switched the mic from hand to hand, waiting for the music to start. As the rap soundtrack began, he lifted the mic, avoiding direct eye contact with the crowd.

For the next three minutes, I listened in stunned silence as the young man rapped his way through his time at our school. He was angry at what he described to be an expectation of conformity, judgment, and even hypocrisy. He was visibly agitated, and at times his lyrics were explicit and inappropriate—but I could sense that, interspersed between the vitriol and exhibitionism, were wounds tender to the touch: *I felt no love, only judgment. No acceptance, only exclusion for not being who you thought I was supposed to be. Is this how God feels about me?*

When he finished, cheers erupted around me while I stood in stunned silence. The illusion I had cheerfully maintained that everyone felt as I did—included, seen, loved, and like they belonged—shattered. In that brief moment of disorientation, the Holy Spirit snuck past any defensiveness I might have felt for my school or church and awoke within me a piercing empathy. Who was this young man, and what had he endured? There was no doubt that many of his choices were questionable, and his posture was angry, even hostile. But what had he undergone? How had he been excluded by the social pressure of our religious enclave? What shame had he been dealt? What judgment had been flung his way?

The campus was abuzz with the controversy. I was distraught, broken by the suffering barely disguised by the young man's rage. A student mentor saw my distress and sat me down. Instead of helping me process my unexpected sensation of empathy and sorrow, she highlighted all the ways his act had done damage to the community. I nodded quietly if only to give the impression of agreement so I could attend more closely to all that was stirring in my heart.

The Spirit gently prompted me: this young man may have misstepped, but he did not fail the community. Rather, the Christian community had failed him. Our welcome had come with strings attached. *Come! Belong to us, but only if you become like us. Belong to us, but leave your otherness at the door. Belong to us, but silence doubt and uncertainty. Belong to us, but do not make us question or reevaluate the status quo.*

Looking back through a more mature, experienced lens, I recognize the toxicity of that young man's behavior. It was a selfish, arrogant way to communicate his experience. I also recognize the importance of welcoming every person without welcoming every behavior in a community, particularly a residential university. However, the anger and hurt on his face are seared into my memory, as well as the roar of the students around me who felt seen by his diatribe. His experience was not unique. In our wayward attempts to distinguish ourselves from culture, we—the church—have become gatekeepers. Frightened by encroaching secularism, we have withheld the opportunity for people to belong to the faith community unless they believe what we determine to be essential, and align their behavior with our standards.

That young man did not need a gatekeeper. He was only too aware of how his behavior prevented his belonging. What he needed was a tour guide—someone to invite him in and show him around the faith, like a host showing a cherished houseguest the bathroom, the snack cupboard, and the bedroom where he can rest for the evening. How might his experience—and the experiences of countless others who have been excluded from belonging because they don't quite have it together—be different had he been allowed to bear witness to a community both radically in love with Jesus and radically committed to embodying the Jesus way of mercy, justice, and compassion, a community far too busy practicing redemptive love to bother with imposing litmus tests on those seeking belonging?

What if the church became such a community of belonging in which everyone were welcomed as I was welcomed—as a treasured, doted-upon pastor's child? What if they were ushered into the family room for conversation and coffee? What if they were allowed to join us for dinner and then tossed a towel to help dry dishes? What if our profound trust in Jesus and the redemptive power of God transformed us into an unafraid, spacious people, unthreatened by and open to the other?

Why Did We Decide to Write This Book as a Team?

Our stories differ, yet we have all found a home in the same denomination. We come from different generations, different parts of the world, and different family backgrounds, yet we all love Jesus, and we all love the unique expression of his body that is our denomination. Through the faithfulness of Jesus followers in local congregations, we have all experienced the transformative love of God and responded to a call to give our lives in service to the church.

Each of us, in our own way, has come to recognize the need for a reorientation in the church. For historical and sociological reasons that we will explore throughout this book, the church has come, mistakenly, to define belonging as the product of agreement upon doctrines and mores. Such a view demands that a person behave and believe like us, religious insiders, before they belong to the fellowship of Christ followers. This confusion has left many feeling alienated and unwelcome among the people of God. It is our hearts' desire to attend to and name the reorienting work of the Spirit stirring among us, the Spirit who invites us to surrender this disordered understanding of belonging and re-embrace the way of Jesus: welcoming people into the fellowship of the church.

As they experience the living Christ through shared life and genuine belonging with believers, lives are changed. Behaviors begin to shift—not *in order* to belong but *because* they already belong. Belief in the resurrected Christ and in God's redemptive purposes for individuals and creation is birthed in hearts.

Deep love for the church motivates this work. Love requires both honesty and hope. It requires that we speak the truth with grace. Love without honesty is hidden under the weight of all that is not said that desperately needs to be addressed. Intimacy is suffocated by uneasy silence for fear that the truth will be too painful, or perhaps unwelcome. Honesty and truth spoken in love throw open the windows to the fresh air that is the Spirit of God, allowing for the possibility of reorientation, healing, and growth.

But speaking the truth honestly and with love must be accompanied by radical hope. Hope is that virtue that waters the ever-growing plant of love. Without hope, love is stagnant. It blossoms for a moment, like a flower in a vase, but ultimately shrivels because it is severed from the life-giving soil of hope. Hope nourishes love and provides a meaningful vision for all that is possible, even when the present feels uncertain and frightening.

With this hope, we want to speak the truth in love to the church. With honesty, we confront the reality that exists in the church—that, in many ways, we have surrendered our vocation as light bearers and wrongfully elevated boundary-keeping to our primary task. Discipleship often has devolved into content acquisition while faith is reduced to cognitive assent. Time and again, the gates of community are guarded against those who differ from us. Those outside the boundaries of the church, those who hunger after that which they cannot name, often continue to starve as insiders die on petty hills of preference and politics.

Sometimes honesty can wound, yet we are not crippled by the pain. We also know that, sometimes, honesty can be used to heal. Strengthened by hope, we look to a vibrant future for the church we love. Our hope is rooted not in a new, shiny method for wringing orthodoxy or orthopraxy out of a few brave souls who happen to wander into our churches. Our hope is rooted in an abiding faith that God will not abandon God's church. God will correct, admonish, reorient, and rectify—but *never abandon*—God's church. We do not fear what lies on the other side of divine redirection. God never orients us away from the status quo without inviting us into a divine-human partnership of reorientation toward something more faithful.

This book is an account of some of that reorientation. It is a dialectical assessment of the church and the ways in which the church has gotten off course, as has happened so many times throughout history. It may be painful and uncomfortable, and perhaps even disorienting—but not without purpose. We also explore God's invitation to return once again to the faithful, open nature of the church that God established. This book is not another surefire method to church growth or a failproof evangelism tool. It is a call to return anew to our identity and vocation as Christ's body, a return to the call to model our life together after our crucified and resurrected Lord. It is a reorientation toward a vision of the church as an inclusive community with hearts set on Jesus.

This is not to suggest that the institutional aspect of the church is unimportant or should cease. Organizations that endure and blossom as fruitful entities into the future require certain structural measures. However, the institutional structure cannot be the primary means by which people come to belong to the fellowship of Jesus followers. As we let go of our mental paradigms on who can belong and who cannot, we joyfully discover the Spirit transforming us into a hospitable people who are grounded in the lordship of Jesus and who are unafraid and free to love and serve the world.

2. FROM A MOVEMENT TO A MONUMENT
When the Bs Shifted

Gustavo

When Jesus said to Peter in Matthew 16:18, "I will build my church, and the gates of Hades will not overcome it," he was talking about the establishment of one the greatest movements humanity would ever experience. In fact, the church started as a movement of people who embraced a gospel that was designated for everyone, everywhere. Upon Christ's death, resurrection, and ascension, and the further commissioning and empowerment of his disciples, the church of Jesus Christ became a movement that, throughout the centuries, has turned the world upside down, as recorded as early as the first century of the life of the church (see Acts 17:6).

This movement started with the premise that the kingdom of God moves when all of us, empowered and mobilized by God's Spirit, embrace the mission to reach everyone, everywhere, so that everyone could join God's moving among themselves in their own setting. I remember reading a quote that defined the passion of the early church to reach everyone. Daniel T. Niles, a Sri Lankan evangelist of the twentieth century, was known for saying that "evangelism is one beggar telling another beggar where to find the bread."[2] This belief that we are all beggars who have, by grace, found the Bread of Life, moved the first-century church to be an evangelistic church that was committed to the mission of God to reach God's entire creation.

That inclusive movement started the movement that we call "the church." Paul emphasized such inclusion when writing to the new believers in Rome (many of whom were gentiles and thus excluded from Judaism). He knew it was ingrained in people to be selective, self-appointed, and exclusive, so he needed to highlight the truth that this new movement, the church of Christ, had been designed for everyone. For Paul, the death and resurrection of Jesus Christ solved the problem of the exclusion of the gentiles from God's plan of redemption: "This righteousness is given through faith in Jesus Christ to all who believe. There is no difference between Jew and Gentile, for all have sinned and fall short of the glory of God, and all are

---

2. Daniel T. Niles, *That They May Have Life* (New York: Harper & Bros, 1951).

justified freely by his grace through the redemption that came by Christ Jesus" (Romans 3:22–24).

So the concept of the church being a place where we can all belong and be accepted as we are is not very radical after all. Throughout the history of the church, this concept has been seen as radical only during those times when the church has been challenged to transition back to a movement from the static monument it can so easily become. During those times God has done something to reshuffle the thinking of the church—every time. Every time God has wanted to redirect the church to refocus on his kingdom, he led his church to return to the basics, to refocus the church on Jesus.

Because of its human dimension, even the first-century church was not exempt from the tension between exclusion and embrace. There are several events of the very early church recorded in the book of Acts that give an account of God's intervention in adjusting the thinking of the church and its leaders. One such event was the Council at Jerusalem in Acts 15, where the movement of God had reached the gentiles and some Jewish believers demanded that the gentiles "be circumcised and required to keep the law of Moses" (v. 5). In a critical decision that changed the course of the church as the movement of God, inspired by God's Spirit, the leaders of the first-century church embraced the new believers—gentiles who had joined the movement in Antioch, Syria, and Cilicia—with the belief that "it is through the grace of our Lord Jesus that we are saved, just as they are" (v. 11). Luke wrote that "it seemed good to the Holy Spirit" for the church "not to burden" the new believers "with anything beyond" the basic requirements of the faith—and not the culture (v. 28). In this way, the movement passed its first test of exclusion.

Everything started with a movement. Movements in the life of the church have happened whenever God's Spirit moved those who were responsive to its prompting. Then, scores of people wanted to join the movement because they identified with the message and the mission that the responsive people proclaimed. But to understand where that movement called "the church" is today, we also need to understand the patterns by which long-lasting movements in the life of the church have operated throughout history. Rebecca Lewis's study of more than a dozen movements in the life of the church that lasted more than a hundred years and impacted hundreds of thousands of people suggests these common patterns among movements:

1. *They were started by a person called by God and compelled by the Holy Spirit.*

2. *Each individual continually sought God for a specific unfolding plan to spread the vision widely.*

3. *The plan resulted in highly committed groups with the same vision that were small and self-replicating.*

4. *The groups engaged in transforming both the individuals and their broader community.*

5. *Institutionalizing or aligning with powers seemed to slow or stop movements.*[3]

Therefore:

Movements happen because everyone who joins them has a sense of belonging and a profound sense of mission.

We move because we belong.

Movements are conglomerates of people who feel they are part of something and who identify with that something.

Movements, however, are not without their messes. Because everyone is welcome in the movement, you naturally have segments of people who are there just for the sake of joining the masses—but they do so without conviction. These are the people who often deviate from the spirit or purpose of the movement, and the church is not exempt. Whether through those who wanted to join the movement for personal gain (see Ananias and Sapphira in Acts 5) or through those who had their own ideas about what the kingdom of God should focus on (see Judas the Zealot, who thought the movement was about earthly struc-

---

3. Rebecca Lewis, "Patterns in Long-Lasting Movements," *Mission Frontiers* (March/April 2020), 8.

tural changes), the movement of the kingdom of God has always attracted some who want to be part of it without a conviction about its purpose.

Those sources of chaos in a movement have been the ones who have justified the need for order—or, as Rebecca Lewis calls it, "institutionalization or alignment." So even the most committed members of a welcoming movement started putting some things in order. They needed to develop methods. It was normal. The problem in the church throughout history has not been the need for or pursuit of order in the midst of chaos. Rather, the problem has been the overemphasis of order at the expense of the heart of the movement.

This is how the movement started to become an organization. Early fathers and mothers needed to regulate the movement and bring order to it. Paul understood that. In his letter to Titus, he reminded him that the reason he had been left behind in Crete was to finish the missional work of the apostle and to bring order to the chaos that had been left behind (1:5). I also understand the need for order and organization: I'm an architect. My graduate studies were in planning; my PhD is in organizational leadership. You may say that I am a straight-line freak: architect, planner, and organizational scholar. In these three formal training programs I learned that the best way to maximize efficiencies and movements is to organize them. In fact, let me tell you a secret: I love the governance documents of my denomination because they help move the mission forward (when we use them to enable mission and not to curtail it). But I also learned during my secular training that these mechanisms of order in the midst of chaos (chaordic thinking) are not the ones that define the movement. They can only facilitate it, and then only when the mechanisms do not overtake or define the mission.

We do need to regulate in the midst of the chaos of a movement. We need to regulate if we want to avoid what happened in Revelation 2–3 with the churches in Pergamum (which compromised the doctrine by allowing paganism into the teachings of the church), Thyatira (which allowed corruption and sexual immorality as normal practices in the life of the church), and Sardis (which pretended to be alive because of activism but was indeed spiritually dead). Sadly, these movement-halting incidents happened within the first century of the life of the church. The movement became tainted by unorthodox outside influence because not everybody who joined the movement really shared, loved, and embraced the heart of the movement as originally established by its founder, Jesus. This damage to the church of Christ inspired the early leaders of the movement to have some methodology and to develop some norms to protect the longevity of the movement.

The problem is not our attempts to reorient chaos through institutional mechanisms. The problem is when mechanisms become more important than the mission and the message. So, through an overemphasis on methods and norms, the church has been transformed from a movement into an organization (or monument) that must be preserved and protected. Thus, our organization becomes more important than the message and the mission. And that's when we get in trouble. In architecture school I learned that form follows function. Structures and organizations must be a means to an end; the end purpose of an organization is not the method. The end purpose of governance documents and norms is to facilitate the mission of God.

This is where change must begin. We are no longer talking about the first-century church. We are talking about the early fathers and mothers of the church—those leaders of the institutional church after the first couple of centuries and beyond—who saw the need for order to prevent chaos but took that need to extremes. Perhaps the best summary of that change came from an article from the University of Africa School of Missiology called "Belonging before Believing." The authors, Mario Weyers and Willem Saayman, describe what happened after the first generation of the movement: "No one who was not a recognized member could participate fully in Christian worship without having passed through formal training for membership, and no one could be baptized who had not been prepared through Catechesis before becoming a member of the Christian congregation; therefore one had to go through a prescribed process of teaching and induction."[4] This process of indoctrination, which was implemented after the first-century church (also known as the New Testament church), was perhaps useful for the proper management of the human dimension of the church. However, it is a process defined as the linear progression of **believing** and **behaving** before **becoming** and, hence, before **belonging**.

The reality is that this paradigm has shaped most of the history of the church since its institutionalization. Of course, throughout its history, the Lord has always found a way to inspire his church and reignite the movement by inspiring his people to reorient. So is this perhaps a time to reorient centuries of monument-driven ecclesiology? Some people may think we are crazy or that we don't care for our beloved denominational home. On the contrary, every time God has wanted to bring about a reorientation of his salvific, missionary work, he brings us back to the basics.

When we study church history, particularly of the generations following the first-century church, we recognize that one of the most essential features in the process of evangelism was the process of catechesis, that process of preparing believers to become members of a Christian community. This, of course,

---

4. Mario Weyers and Willem Saayman, "'Belonging before Believing': Some Missiological Implications of Membership and Belonging in a Christian Community," *Verbum et Ecclesia* 34(1), Art. #834, p. 1.

was different from the teachings and practices of the first-century church, and we have to make this distinction. After the first century, and ever since the church became institutionalized, this is the model we have been given. The paradigm in which we were formed and in which the church has been comfortably operating finds its roots in the catechism model as synonymous to disciple-making. This is what we have become experts at: our work is to lead people to believe. Therefore, we emphasize that evangelism is about leading people to believe.

I once watched a well-known Christian program on television where the teacher started with the question, "How do people know that you are a follower of Christ?" Not unlike many of our great contemporary evangelistic thinkers, the speaker emphasized that everything started with the process of believing. He then went on to say, "As soon as you believe there are certain behaviors that demonstrate that you believe." The rest of the teaching hour focused on the behaviors that identify a believer of Jesus Christ. Even more interesting was that I agreed with everything he said because everything he said was exactly what I learned when I became a believer at age nineteen.

So the expectation is that if you believe, you have to behave in a certain way, and if you don't behave this way, then you're not a believer. Just as with the catechism model of the early church, your right behaviors then allow you to become part of the community of believers—who, of course, also behave accordingly. At the end—and only at the end—you finally belong. This is, in summary, the existing paradigm of most churches in modern Christianity. First, you **believe**. Then, you show that you are a believer by the way you **behave**. Once you behave, you can **become** an official member of the congregation (or the denomination, the community of believers with an agreed-upon set of covenants, the movement). After you become a member, then, and only then, you **belong**.

This is the established order of modernity. This is the established order of centuries of Christendom. This is the paradigm in which most of us have been trained and in which we operate as a church. This is what brought us here. This is how the church has, at times in its history, lost its way.

Jerry

How do we engage a culture that has become deaf to our message and that has grown disappointed at our non-inclusive methodology? All the evangelistic methods I learned in my ministerial training were message-driven. They started with what you believe. I remember, as a college student, going door to door with a memorized plan to get people to quickly understand that they were in cosmic peril and that, even though I had just met them on their front porch, I had the answer and the path to their personal salvation. Here's the thing. I still believe I did have the answer for them. I believe that Jesus is absolutely the Way, the Truth, and the Life, but was starting with what you believe the best way to communicate this good news? My personal experience with Jehovah's Witnesses and Mormon missionaries gives me firsthand experience with what it feels like to answer the door when a stranger is interested in changing the metanarrative of my life with a prepackaged presentation and a tract.

It would be a mistake to assume that this method *never* results in life change in the lives of broken people—it has, and it does. There are inspiring testimonies of divine appointments that have occurred on doorsteps. But the research is in, and unfortunately it tells us that this is not the way the vast majority of people are open to spiritual conversation. Most of us are not eager to engage with strangers giving advice about what we should think and believe. I learned in junior high that you can't kiss someone who is leaning away from you, and all indicators are that, when it comes to the church, the culture is not leaning in.

While pointing out the inherent weaknesses in some evangelistic strategies, it is important not to create a philosophical fool's choice, where we falsely believe we are forced to choose between only two options. Clearly both in Scripture and experience there are illustrations of someone responding to the gospel when first hearing the message from a stranger. The story of Philip and the Ethiopian eunuch in Acts 8 is a good example. But it also seems clear that the disciples had not yet figured out who Jesus was when he said "follow me," and they did (see Matthew 4:19–22; 9:9; Mark 1:16–20; 2:14;

Luke 5:27–28; John 1:43). It wasn't until much later that he asked them, "Who do you say I am?" (Matthew 16:15; Mark 8:29; Luke 9:20). Even though they *belonged* to his inner circle, what they *believed* was still being formed in them.

We should be open to and aware of moments when the Spirit would lead us to speak faith-producing words into the lives of people we've just met, but this is not how most people come to believe and change the way they are living. It is much more common that people come to faith as they walk with a friend—this was true for eleven of the twelve disciples and has always been the most effective method of evangelism and discipleship.

I have a friend with a forceful personality who often leads people she has just met in the sinner's prayer and then posts about it on Facebook. Some of her stories are inspiring, and I admire her boldness in presenting Jesus and leaving the results up to God, but I wonder how those new converts do at becoming *disciples*. Was the telemarketer she prayed with "born again"? Did the prayer over the phone result in a change of behavior and belief? I obviously don't know, but I do know that they were treated with compassion and kindness—something telemarketers don't often receive, even from professing Christians.

Birth is a beautiful thing, but babies need a lot of nurturing if they are to survive. I do not want to limit the work of the Spirit, but Scripture and experience tell us that Christian community—the church—is an essential part of salvation. The Western church's focus on the individual and personal aspects of the Christian experience seems to be a misreading of much of Paul's instruction to believers in the places where he planted Christian communities. While conversion is always a personal experience, discipleship never is. Belonging to the community is what it means to be Christian. Simply stated, they will know we are Christian by our love—and love doesn't happen in isolation.

So there are at least four aspects to the Christian experience that can be expressed in a simple four-word alliteration: Believe, Behave, Become, and Belong. Because the Christian life is a journey more than a list of accomplishments, these four aspects of the Christian life are all being developed simultaneously and should not be seen as steps on the stairway to heaven. I am always in the process of understanding more clearly what I **believe**, striving to **behave** more like Jesus, and deepening the conviction that the gospel story is the story where I **belong**, all while **becoming** more comfortable with myself and useful to others. But is one of these Bs a first step?

Stephanie

It is important to understand our terms in context to assess where we have been and where we hope to go. The words "believe, behave, become, and belong" can be interpreted in a multitude of ways. Without clarity, unnecessary conflict and frustration may arise. Let's conclude this chapter about the current paradigm of the church with clear definition of the terms as currently understood to better prepare us to engage with a new paradigm in subsequent chapters.

In our current paradigm, orthodoxy (right **belief**) is the first gate to belonging. In order to move toward belonging to a Christian community, a person must give *intellectual assent* to a certain set of doctrines. To give intellectual assent is to acknowledge that you agree with a concept and believe it to be true. It has no implication of transformation. To enter the community, individuals assent to a specific set of doctrines, some universal and some context-specific.

The subsequent gate to belonging is behavior and the idea that right belief should lead to orthopraxy (right **behavior**). This transformation is measured by the community, usually by a set of specific litmus tests. If behavior is not changed within a certain time period and in a certain way as determined by the community, this second gateway to belonging remains closed. The challenge with this approach is that these expectations are often unspoken. It is assumed that a new believer seeking transformation should know and be able to conform to the community standards. As with belief, the behavioral expectations of a local church are both universal and context-specific. Everyone would agree that murder and adultery are out of bounds. However, local culture adds to those expectations additional contextual behavioral expectations around other things that have far more to do with culture than with Jesus's teaching.

The final gate before passing into belonging is becoming. Once orthodoxy and orthopraxy have been established, a person **becomes** a member of the body of Christ at large, and of a local community. Membership entails affirming doctrines and conforming to a specific way of being in the world as understood by the covenants of Scripture and the polity of the community to which the person desires to belong.

Finally, after entering through these previous three gates, a person may **belong** to the church with all its rights, privileges, and responsibilities. But it is a fragile belonging that is contingent on continued conformity. Belonging can be rescinded if any standard of belief or behavior is questioned, whether universal or context-specific.

Many will likely feel this to be an extreme take on the traditional paradigm, but the reality is that most churches already operate on a spectrum between the inherited tradition and the new paradigm we will explore in the following chapters. However, in our decades of combined ministry experience, we three authors have come to see the damage caused by withholding belonging from those seeking after God, even those who cannot name their experience as such. It is our hope to reshuffle this process to reflect the radical inclusion of God, rooted in grace, mutuality, and hope.

3. TOWARD A REORIENTATION
Reshuffling the Bs

Gustavo

Is there a better, more faithful way? The narrative of the gospel allows generous space for those who first need to belong before they are ready to fully believe, behave, or become. This important reality is part of the paradigmatic shift we submit to you. We introduce this reality not because of a desire to challenge the status quo but because we really believe that the gospel story allows us in this generation, after centuries of Christendom, to re-Jesus the church, in a similar way that the Lord has allowed his church to be reoriented in various chapters of its history.[5]

---

5. While much writing has happened since the mid-1960s about reemphasizing the centrality of Jesus in the church, the term "re-Jesus" became more ingrained in contemporary ecclesiological circles through the work of Michael Frost and Alan Hirsch in their 2008 book *ReJesus: A Wild Messiah for a Missional Church*.

Perhaps, then, this is a good time to reorder the Bs. In reordering the Bs, we can be part of a movement where everybody belongs, allowing room for many to believe and behave like Christlike disciples so that many would become part of our faith communities and part of the global church.

We deeply love the denomination we serve, and we pray that, without distorting or eliminating the theological and covenantal agreements of our faith community, we would be able to reorient the order of some of the contemporary ecclesiological processes to abide by the model established by Jesus, the head of the church. In this reorder, everybody belongs— just as they are, with their idiosyncrasies, with their background and baggage, and even with their personal agendas that may be distant from the agenda of the kingdom of God. Everybody belongs because, like on the classic show *Cheers*, "Sometimes you want to go where everybody knows your name."

In the original model established by Jesus, everybody **belongs** first. Then, ideally, everybody **believes**. Next, everybody **behaves** because everyone's lives have been transformed. Because everybody behaves, everybody **becomes** a member of the community. That's the ideal scenario.

We are going to present it again: People join the movement of followers of the teachings of Christ because they **belong** and have found a community that allows them to journey. These people come to

believe because they find truth in the teachings, the power, and the person of Christ. Their **behaviors** demonstrate their life as a new creation in Christ. Finally, they grow with the community to **become** like Christ and, in the process, become part of those faith communities because they agree, espouse, and are willing to promote the doctrines and the agreed-upon covenants of each specific group. That's the scenario that Christ painted for his disciples when he commissioned them.

We do not propose abolition of the doctrinal and covenantal agreements that define our faith communities and denominations. We all believe in doctrine and covenant! In our specific case, we believe that the tenets of our denomination—described as Christian, holiness, and missional—are biblical and are rooted in good orthodoxy and orthopraxy. We believe that the ecclesiological instructions passed on from the first-century church to us today are still legitimate and relevant. The major reorientation shift we propose is to move the belonging part to the very beginning instead of the very end of the discipleship journey, as it was distorted by centuries of institutionalism.

Pursuant to this reorientation, we would like to suggest some paradigm[shifts. This whole idea of belonging before believing means that we need to re-shift and study one B at a time.

∫ Stephanie: A paradigm is a way of seeing. It is a set of lenses that inform how we perceive the world around us. It is not a cut-and-paste method. It requires contextualization, critical thinking, and individualized application.

First Paradigm Shift: Belonging Is Foundational

For Jesus, everyone was welcomed to journey with him, to listen to his teachings, and to belong to his followership. In fact, when he called the disciples, he didn't originally call them to believe in him. His calling to the disciples was a call to followership (see Matthew 4:18–22; 9:9; Mark 1:16–20; 2:14; Luke 5:27; John 1:43).∫ In every encounter Jesus had with the multitudes, he didn't limit his presence, his teachings, or his miracles only to those who believed. His all-inclusive love was available to everyone who—regardless of their past or their present expectations—was willing to listen, to come, to follow.

Several years ago, I had the privilege to write in a book edited by Leonard Sweet about the untold story of God's global awakening. In its introduction, Len describes this all-inclusive loving heart that moved Jesus to welcome everyone: "Jesus greeted everyone he encountered as the original, sacramental, transfigural apple of his eye. His imagination shows us the image of God in every person."[6] The premise here is that, because everyone is made in the image of God and because God's plan is to reconcile creation to God's self through Christ, then everybody belongs. Everybody.

> ∫ Stephanie: The disciples belonged before they understood or believed in Jesus as the Son of God. According to the Gospels, they were invited to live in a certain way—change their behavior—even before believing. While belonging should lead the way in the process of discipleship, what follows should be allowed to unfold organically. For some, belief will follow belonging. For others, changed behaviors practiced in community will precede belief as they grow in the knowledge of Christ.

---

6. Leonard Sweet and James O. Davis, *We Are the Church: The Untold Story of God's Global Awakening* (Orlando: Billion Soul Publishing, 2014), xxix.

In Jesus we learn that, while the plan of salvation is for everyone who believes (John 3:16), Jesus gave everyone the opportunity to journey with him, listen to him, explore his teachings, experience his miracles and his power, and discover the depth of his love. As a result of journeying with him, some believed and entered into God's plan of salvation. Others didn't believe and therefore did not access the blessing of his salvific plan. Nevertheless, Jesus never pushed away those who, in spite of journeying with him, chose not to believe.

We need to make sure we are not minimizing the value of believing in Christ as the central tenet of God's plan of salvation for humanity. The plan hasn't changed. In John 3:16–17, Jesus spells out the plan with clarity, eloquence, and purpose: Jesus came to save the whole world. Salvation is directly connected to and dependent upon believing in him. Nobody should change that, nor can they. We are trying to reinforce, however, that Jesus allowed everyone to come to him. His teachings and practices emphasized the reality that everyone was welcome to follow him, to listen to him, and to be part of his crowd. Everyone belonged. Yes, it was hoped that everyone would believe, but that was the gift. Belonging was the setting.

"Large crowds from Galilee, the Decapolis, Jerusalem, Judea and the region across the Jordan followed him" (Matthew 4:25).

"But the crowds learned about it and followed him. He welcomed them and spoke to them about the kingdom of God, and healed those who needed healing" (Luke 9:11).

Some followed him because of his fame or reputation or because they thought there was something material they could get out of his ministry (John 6:2).

One of the common threads in these stories is that there were large crowds that followed Jesus. Whether they were interested in his teachings, his miracles, his persona, or all of the above, Jesus ministered to and welcomed them regardless of their intentions or personal backgrounds. Of the thousands who followed him, very few were believers (even among his inner circle). This did not keep Jesus from loving them and ministering to their physical and emotional needs. Jesus went even beyond the everyone-is-welcome attitude modeled in the kingdom of God. He specifically reached out to those who had been intentionally marginalized and excluded by the religious or social norms of his time. The table of belonging was extended to:

- The children: While his disciples became annoyed by the presence of children around Jesus, he reminded them that "the kingdom of heaven belongs to such as these" (Matthew 19:15).
- The detestable tax collector: While tax collectors were despised by both religious leaders and society at large because of their corrupt

practices, at least two of them were welcomed thanks to the grace of Jesus: Matthew/Levi, who became one of the Twelve as well as a Gospel writer (Matthew 9:9–12; Mark 2:13–17), and Zacchaeus, who changed his behavior the moment Jesus told him he belonged (Luke 19:1–10).

- The wretched sinful woman: While at the house of a religious leader, Jesus was anointed by "a woman in that town who lived a sinful life" (Luke 7:37). While the religious leader admonished Jesus's poor judgment and lack of discernment for allowing a sinful woman to approach him, Jesus highlighted the value of the woman's faith over the religious man's traditions and prejudices (Luke 7:36–50).

- The condemned adulterous woman: In this crucial story that juxtaposed the reality of the law and the salvific power of love, Jesus intentionally chose not to violate the law by overlooking the woman's sin while at the same time being consistent in his mission to save what was lost. His reaction, which was full of justice and love, showed his gentleness and forgiveness while he invited the woman to renounce a reckless lifestyle. Jesus welcomed her, loved her, and forgave her (John 8:1–11).

- The untouchable lepers: When approached by a leper, Jesus didn't push him away or react as if he were afraid of the man. Instead,

∫ *Stephanie: Churches frequently tout the "everyone is welcome" tagline. However, the belonging we offer is often anemic. First, we often presume it is the outsiders' responsibility to come to us. If they come, we will be kind, but we often balk at the thought of going where people without Christ spend their time. Second, there are often unspoken expectations about behavior and appearance, some of which make belonging a nonstarter. A visitor is dressed inappropriately? Send someone to talk to that lady about her shirt, or she'll need to go. A person lives in a way that contradicts our convictions? Make sure he knows our feelings on the matter. The belonging we offer is too often passive and conditional.*

† *Jerry: This welcoming focus places responsibility on those who are mature members of the fellowship. Their lives must evidence the fruit of the Spirit. By example they will hold the crown over the heads of those who are seeking until they grow into it. This is how Jesus formed his disciples.*

he touched him and healed him (Matthew 8:3–4).

- The marginalized Samaritan woman: While conventional wisdom and religious codes prohibited a good Jewish rabbi from setting foot on Samaritan soil—not to mention talking to a woman—Jesus had to go to Samaria and share the good news with the Samaritan woman at the well, who in turn shared it with her whole community (John 4:1–42).

In Jesus's vision of a transformed and redeemed creation, everyone was welcome because everyone was created in his own image, and he accepted everyone as his follower. That's why the first-century church imitated Christ's welcoming attitude. Paul wrote to the Romans reminding them to do the same thing: "Accept one another, then, just as Christ accepted you, in order to bring praise to God" (Romans 15:7).

This is where the heart of the mission is. Not everyone who followed Jesus believed in him. But that did not keep him from ministering to them. Everyone was welcome to follow him. This must be an essential part of the DNA of Christ's church. While not everyone may believe, and many of those who come may not fit what we understand as acceptable to the fellowship, everyone *must* be welcomed to the fellowship of the followers.∫†

One of the paradoxes that has challenged Christians throughout the centuries is the balance between the main purpose of Christ's incarnation, death, and resurrection, and the means by which that message is shared. On one hand, we all know and recognize that the main purpose of God's mission is that we all believe and are justified by faith in Jesus Christ for present and eternal salvation (Romans 10:11–13). On the other hand, we also need to recognize that some will choose not to believe. This shouldn't keep us from allowing everyone to make their choice. Our role is to open our arms to everyone so they can come in contact with the person of Jesus on their own terms. Our job is to set the stage for everybody to belong to the fellowship of the followers. As the artwork piece in my daughter's room says, "Not all those who wander are lost."[7] It is not our job to define who is lost but to allow them to journey and seek so they can have a personal encounter with Jesus, with whom everyone is welcome.

David Putman summarizes this paradigm in his book on discipleship: "We were created with the need for belonging, and if the church is to be relevant, the first need we should meet is the need for community. . . . It is impossible for us to be the church God had in mind if we do not offer authentic, loving, warm environments where people can belong in healthy community. Being a missional follower of Jesus means offering the disconnected a place to belong,

---

7. J. R. R. Tolkien, *The Fellowship of the Ring* (London: George Allen & Unwin, 1954).

understanding that belonging can be a significant step toward believing."[8]

Second Paradigm Shift: While Everyone Belongs, Some Will Believe

Once we set the stage for everyone to belong, we need to understand that some, though not necessarily all, will come to believe. Jesus taught the disciples this reality in a very clear way. John 6:60–69 tells us the story of the time when Jesus acknowledged to his followers that following him was not enough—they needed to believe. "The words I have spoken to you—they are full of the Spirit and life. Yet there are some of you who do not believe" (vv. 63b–64a). He even challenged his followers and his closer disciples to move from following him to believing in him. Some made the choice to leave him while others, when confronted with the life-giving truth of Jesus's life and message, decided to affirm their belief (vv. 66–68).

While setting the atmosphere for everyone to belong is an intentional practice of the church (both individually and corporately), believing is a more intentional exchange between those who belong to the fellowship of the followers and Christ himself—through the work of the Holy Spirit. That's why not everyone who belongs believes.

---

8. David Putman, *Breaking the Discipleship Code: Becoming a Missional Follower of Jesus* (Nashville: B&H Publishing Group), 71.

David Putman helps us understand the difficulty of this reality. For him, today—as it was in the time of Jesus—many circles are embracing Jesus, but in a rather self-defined form of spirituality, "they are embracing him as *a* way rather than *the* way."[9] For Putman, not every follower turns into a believer because believing requires time, a safe place for followers to search, and nonjudgmental relationships that allow the follower to find the truth. However, they affirm that, just like in Jesus's time, being exposed to the truth in love doesn't always result in followers becoming believers because they don't feel ready to fully accept and embrace Jesus as the only way to the Father.

As a church, we must realize that, even among the closest followers of Jesus, there were some who didn't believe, and this reality did not distract Jesus from his redemptive mission. Even his brothers, who grew up with him, didn't believe in him (John 7:5). Thomas did not believe until after he saw the fulfillment of the promise of resurrection from the dead (John 20). Even many of his disciples after months and even years journeying with him didn't completely believe until they had their spiritual eyes—blinded by merely human concerns—opened (Mark 8:22–26).

What this means for the church is that our primary role is to set a witnessing environment that allows people to encounter Jesus on their journey and, as they

∫ Stephanie: To be non-judgmental is not the same as having no opinion or convictions. Rather, it means suspending our own assessment for a moment in time in the hope of creating space for another person to grow, learn, and think without the heavy cloud of our desires blocking out the sun of God's always-on-time revelation.

9. Putman, *Breaking the Discipleship Code*, 62.

† Jerry: I remember the lyrics of a song from my early days in youth ministry: "If there is a doubter in the crowd, we ask you not to leave." Sometimes, by the inconsistencies of our own lives and our natural tendency to defend our point of view, we drive people with honest questions out of the fellowship before they have the opportunity to find their own faith.

∫ Stephanie: It is impossible to escape cultural nuance. We are always standing in a particular place with a particular history and worldview. Some things that are considered morally wrong among the people of Papua New Guinea are morally neutral to Americans, and vice versa. Context matters. However, the ultimate authority on behavior and whether certain commands are binding for all times in all places is Scripture—read discerningly in the company of the historical church, guided by the Holy Spirit.

encounter Jesus, pray for the witness of the Holy Spirit to allow followers to claim, like Peter, "You are the Messiah, the Son of the living God" (Matthew 16:16).

Paul was aware of this kingdom reality. During his ministry in Athens, he spent days in conversations with philosophers and thinkers of his time. While being open to their context and their cultural realities, Paul found a way to expose them to Jesus. Many scorned him while others found the conversation interesting. Only a few believed. That was enough for the church in Athens to be planted. Everyone was welcome. Few believed. And that was okay.†

Third Paradigm Shift: All Believers Are Changed

The third shift for the church is the need to revisit the role behaviors play in defining a believer. In the Christendom model, the early fathers and mothers developed lists of behaviors, some of them biblically grounded and some of them cultural, as evidence of new life in Christ. Unfortunately, while many of these behaviors *were* rooted in Scripture, some of them were taken out of context and some were tainted by the cultural nuances of the places where the church ministered.∫ Because of that, some of the cultural behaviors were presented as scriptural, and some scriptural behaviors were ill-defined out of context, leaving the behavioral dimension of the church in the hands of the institutions and away from biblical orthodoxy and orthopraxy. Further, because of the overemphasis on external behaviors as a sign of inward transformation, many followers incrementally acquired and publicly exhibited the prescribed behaviors without having been born again as true believers of Christ. This externally focused definition of a believer caused the proliferation of nominal believers—followers of Christ who practiced the rituals of the religion without a true faith relationship with Christ.

Because of the power of peer pressure and social influence in movements, behaviors cannot be the main measure of internalization of the movement's belief system. Religion without a personal relationship results in behaviors without conviction. This is what Jesus faced during his ministry from the religious leaders—and even some of his followers. When chastised by the religious leaders about some behavioral practices that broke with the tradition of the elders, Jesus admonished them with the prophecy against nominal religion: "These people honor me with their lips, but their hearts are far from me. They worship me in vain; their teachings are merely human rules" (Matthew 15:8–9, quoting Isaiah 29:13). This narrative highlights for us the inherited problem of overemphasizing behaviors as the main evidence of a disciple's belief. In fact, being a disciple of Christ is not simply behavioral modification.[†ʃ] There are many stories in contemporary Christianity where people join a church and start behaving according to the behavioral patterns of the other congregants, not because they have been transformed or because they believe in Christ but because they have either

† Jerry: The fruit of focusing on modification of behavior first is almost always a cold legalism that sucks the joy out of the entire fellowship of believers. This usually results in layer after layer of expectations being applied with the hope that, by perfecting performance, peace and joy will result—but it will not.

ʃ Stephanie: Changed behavior is neither salvific nor ought it be the primary measure of one's relationship with God. However, let's leave room for changed behavior as a gateway to belief. Experiencing life change in the company of believers has on many occasions led people to commit their lives to Christ.

absorbed the behaviors or because they have been pressured to behave like the rest. When the alcoholic stops drinking or the addict stops using, the church plays a positive social role, similar to programs like Alcoholics Anonymous or Celebrate Recovery—but this doesn't mean that those with new behaviors are indeed believers.

Paul wrote to the church in Corinth that being a disciple of Christ goes beyond new behaviors. For Paul, a true believer in Christ is compelled by the love of Christ, convinced about the eternal value of his atonement, transformed as a new creation, and commissioned to appeal to others about God's saving and perfecting love (2 Corinthians 5:14–20). In Jesus's model, behavioral changes are preceded by a deep sense of belief and an intentional act of repentance. The Gospel of Mark records the first statements of Jesus's ministry and purpose with the announcement that "the kingdom of God has come near. Repent and believe the good news!" (1:15). Repentance and belief go together because if we believe that Jesus Christ is our Lord and Savior (belief by faith), we also have a changed state of mind about our sins and behaviors (repentance), and these behaviors are continually transformed by the Holy Spirit, who guides us to abundant life.

The idea here is not to dismiss the transformational power of salvation in a person's behavior, but not all those who behave according to the traditions and practices of Christianity are indeed believers unless they have been born again (believed and repented, as Jesus proclaimed). Conversely, one cannot claim that he or she is a believer without tangible evidence of a transformed life that has exchanged the behaviors of the flesh for the fruit of the Spirit. When behaviors are the prescriptions of faith—instead of natural descriptions that flow from a changed life—we find ourselves in the midst of, among other things, generational tensions when one generation pushes behaviors according to their beliefs while the other counterpunches by pushing their beliefs to be reshaped according to their behaviors. Hence, behaviors are not the landmark of belief. Transformed lives are.∫

Fourth Paradigm Shift: Becoming Is Universal and Institutional

In the process of writing this book, we grew increasingly concerned about the misunderstanding the contemporary church has with the term "becoming." For some, becoming has an institutional dimension that is primarily related to membership in a faith community, whether a local church or a denomination. In this case, a believer's becoming is considered a privilege from the community, whereby they have completed the entire process of indoctrination (or catechism), have expressed their agreement with the agreed-upon covenants, polity, and doctrines, and have expressed their desire to join the community. Once these mutually agreed requirements are met (the believers' fulfillment of the requirements as well as the community's recognition of such fulfillment),

∫ Stephanie: What's the difference between changed behaviors and a transformed life? It's not a matter of degree but of motivation and source. If the motivation is social conformity or pressure from a community of faith, the changed behavior will remain an external adjustment and will fall away once the pressure influencing the behavior is removed from one's life. Change born out of love for God and others is evidence of a life that is being transformed by Christ.

† *Jerry: The desire to join a local church can be motivated by something other than discipleship for both laity and clergy. For some, membership equals a spiritual blessing with salvific benefits. "I'm a member of the church, so I'm good with God." For clergy, receiving people into membership can be a validation of their value as a pastor. The number of members in a local church is one of the metrics for success in ministry. "Our church is adding new members, which means I am successful at my vocation." Both motivations miss the mark and subvert the mission.*

then the believers are granted membership status and officially *become* an active part of the community with all the expected privileges and obligations.†

This dimension of becoming is acceptable and necessary for the church as an institution. Like with any living organism that finds its mechanisms for natural community structure and formation, the church as an institution and its various organizational expressions need such mechanisms for believers to join. This, however, is an exercise of mutuality. The church defines its agreed-upon mores, covenants, and doctrines, and believers choose to adopt and embrace them as part of their institutional becoming.

The other, deeper, meaning of the term "becoming" is universal, and is rooted in the biblical instructions to make Christlike disciples. In this universal sense, becoming represents the developmental nature of discipleship beyond external behaviors. It represents the level of growth and maturity of the believer to attain the stature and measure of Christ. Scripture calls this process of becoming more Christlike "sanctification." Sanctification as Christlikeness means embodying God's presence in this physical world, being a completely devoted channel through which God can work to accomplish his mission, and recovering our relational nature so others long for the relationship with God and others that they see in us.[10]

10. Timothy Crutcher, *Becoming Human Again: A Biblical Primer on Entire Sanctification* (independently published, 2020), 86–89.

The fact that these two interpretations of "becoming" are part of our reality requires that we develop a clear understanding of both and that the church learns to identify the natural tension of both interpretations and their application in our daily life both as believers and as members of the Christian community we have joined.

To summarize Jesus's original design as it applies to the church in our generation, this paradigmatic reorientation can be stated as follows:

1. Everyone belongs to the fellowship of the followers. The role of the church is to create an environment where everyone feels welcomed into the fellowship.

2. The main purpose of the fellowship is for people to experience a personal encounter with Jesus. This encounter with Jesus will prompt many to repent and believe. Some will not believe, but that doesn't take away the mission of the church to welcome them and to present them to Jesus.

3. Some will behave because of the influence of the believers, even without being believers themselves. However, all those who believe will display a new behavior by way of a transformed life.

4. Some transformed believers will choose to become part of the community because they feel compelled by the fellowship, the covenants, the doctrines, and the requirements

of the institutional church as defined by the denomination or local church (the agreed-upon values). For whatever reason, some may choose not to become members. This doesn't disqualify them as believers or even as part of the fellowship. This decision only takes away the privileges bestowed to those who choose to become part of the community (for instance, some churches require membership for those who wish to take part in congregational votes or serve on boards or in other leadership roles).

5. Every believer should strive to become a mature disciple, attaining to the whole measure of the fullness of Christ.

While we have attempted to describe the various stages in the life of a follower, it is important to note that the process is not linear because it is dependent on God's sovereignty and prevenient grace. It is also dependent on a follower's free will and the conditions surrounding each follower's journey. Under God's prevenient grace, some believers have believed before they belonged—like the man in the crowd in Mark 9:17–24. Others have belonged for a long time without believing—even some of the disciples of Jesus. Others have displayed Christian behaviors without being believers, while still others, having made a declaration of faith in Christ, continue to struggle with the internal strife of their behaviors (Romans 7:14–20). And, of course, God's sovereignty has the power to transform individuals instantly from a state of sin and desperation to a state of full surrender, victory, and service.

Jerry

All the evangelism methods I learned in my preparation and early years of ministry were built around the assertion that believing was the first step into the Christian life and the door to the fellowship of the church. An appeal can be made to numerous places in Scripture and centuries of church history that validate this approach. The jailer in Philippi asks Paul and Silas, "What must I do to be saved?" Their answer is, "Believe in the Lord Jesus, and you will be saved" (Acts 16:30, 31). The Four Spiritual Laws, the Roman Road, Evangelism Explosion, and even the Billy Graham Crusades were all centered around leading people to believe gospel truth that would result in a personal salvation experience. The point is not to argue that the goal of evangelism isn't an encounter with God centered in orthodox understanding and correct theology. The question is, in a post-Christian society where the church culture of past generations is not even a memory for most of Gen Z and millennials and where Christianity is held suspect in the minds of many, is believing the place to *start* a conversation that leads to faith? Is there anything about the way Jesus connected with people who became his disciples that could give us an answer?

My first experiences as a pastor were all centered around ministry to youth. The idea of belonging

∫ *Stephanie: This kind of incarnational ministry and courageous going forth in the world is essential for ministry in our contemporary world. However, if it is reduced to a method, just another tool to win souls, those we seek to love will sniff out what feels like inauthenticity. The belonging we offer might feel conditional. Incarnational ministry is faithful when it holds the outcomes of ministry loosely in full trust in the Spirit's power to transform.*

before believing was deeply rooted in the methodology I picked up from mentors and then taught when I had the opportunity to train younger leaders. We believed then, and I still believe now, that the gospel message is more incarnational than propositional. Because the students we wanted to reach weren't just the ones already in our churches, we recognized that we would need to *go* where they were and engage with them.∫ Until I was forty, when I changed the focus of my ministry, I spent a lot of my time in the community getting to know students and genuinely taking an interest in their lives. I did have an agenda. I did believe, and still do believe, that people who put their trust in Jesus find the way, the truth, and the life—that just isn't where the conversation starts. This approach opened a lot of doors. By being truly interested in the lives of students and those who worked with them, I was welcomed into places that would normally have been closed to me. I was in the locker room and on the sidelines as a local high school football team took the field to play in the state championship. I was a guest speaker in classes and frequently spoke to all-school assemblies. On a couple of occasions, I was used by administrations to encourage teachers and, once, to help resolve a conflict with an entire middle school staff.

More than twenty years have passed, and the culture has become increasingly skeptical of Christianity in general and pastors in particular, but I know this method still works. Several of our churches in western Washington have developed strong relationships with local schools by asking good questions, listening before assuming, and helping instead of criticizing. The culture is not going to change because we strongly condemn what we oppose and write it on Facebook.

Belonging is a bridge with two-way traffic. Yelling at people about the benefits of my side of the river is unlikely to result in them taking an excursion across the bridge. We need to travel to their side before they are likely to embrace what we believe about the Jesus way to live. I don't have to manipulate the text at all to see that this was the approach Jesus used. He didn't gain a reputation for being the friend of sinners by spending all his time in the synagogue huddled with the scribes and Pharisees. Simply put, we need to go to them before we invite people to come to us.

As I turned forty, my focus of ministry shifted from youth and college to leading a congregation. Although my assignment changed, my underlying philosophy of ministry did not. I still believed the traffic must flow both ways if we hope to be effective at seeing people come to faith in Jesus. Everyone has had that uncomfortable feeling of being somewhere they don't belong. Even if the food is great, attending someone else's family reunion is always going to be a bit awkward. If a person's first exposure to the gospel is in a large group meeting or an in-depth theological discussion, it seems unlikely the response will be (for more than a precious few), "Now *this* is where I belong." Finding places in the community where we can belong and build friendships around common interests makes the door of the church seem far less foreign and much more inviting. For seventeen years on my way to church, I drove by the Moose Lodge and never once went in. I didn't know any moose. Now, if Bullwinkle had invited me to go in with him, that would have been a different story. It doesn't matter how large the crowd—if I'm with a friend, I'm not alone.

As a first principle, belonging is only a concept until it is a relationship. I'm a member of Costco, but I would never think of a big warehouse store as the place where I *belong*. I belong where I am known and accepted, where I can be myself and know what's expected, where I can contribute, where I'm loved. Sometimes it seems desperate churches try to add members like collecting Facebook friends, where the goal can be more about status than connection. In these cases, both believing and belonging are less than authentic, and the result is not Christlike disciples or sustainable Christian communities.

Belonging gives context to our faith.

Stephanie

Heidi was an active participant on a music worship team I led early in my vocational ministry journey. She had recently married a long-time member of the church and quickly found a way to serve. However, whether she was a Christian remained unclear to everyone. It did not take long to recognize that Heidi had come from a broken, dysfunctional home with a different understanding of appropriate behavior. She regularly dropped profanities during rehearsal and often wore clothing that revealed more than most were comfortable with.

Sarah, a member of the church staff, finally took me aside. "She is way out of line. Can't you see that? Her clothes are obscene, and she is on the platform every week." While her approach was unkind, her assessment was not wrong. I was left with the task of having a difficult conversation with a person I knew was still exploring the boundaries of faith.

I met Heidi at a local coffee shop. I listened as she told me about her background and current life goals. I was eager to get to know her but also wanted to find a way to bring up the Issue. I failed at every attempt. There was simply no way to do this subtly. I took a deep breath, steeling myself to say a hard thing. Before I could begin, Heidi spoke again. "My mom won't come to church when she visits. She says she has nothing to wear. I told her, 'Mom, it doesn't matter. At our church, you can wear anything and belong.'"

I was silenced. Hot tears filled my eyes. Thank you, Spirit, for guarding my mouth. I returned to Sarah and said I would not be raking Heidi over the coals for her clothing and that we would be welcoming her exactly as she was.

Over the next several years, I had the privilege of watching Heidi blossom into a flourishing follower of

Jesus. She consistently found ways to serve others and gave her life away that others might come to know the acceptance she had found in Christ and in Christ's body. As she immersed herself in the fellowship of believers and was welcomed without reserve, her behavior changed notably. Conversely, Sarah moved on from her position and withdrew from the congregation in increasing degrees.

A commitment to belonging before believing and behaving is not simple or without struggle. It is messy and complicated. But a decision must be made: are we more interested in conformity and our own comfort, or are we willing to do what it takes to foster a culture in which a person like Heidi can belong? Will we have eyes to see God stirring in a soul, or will we, like Sarah, be too distracted by a life yet unredeemed?

Creating policies to cultivate this culture is wrong-headed from the start. You cannot legislate faithfulness. Faithfulness is only born of an entire-heart surrender in full trust that God is at work in ways we cannot see. Cultivating a culture of belonging is difficult soul work for leaders and laity alike, but it is a faithful expression of obedience to our Lord Jesus, who welcomed us without condition.

4. WHAT DOES BELONGING BEFORE BELIEVING LOOK LIKE?

Jerry

At the Hillside Church in Kent, Washington, it is not unusual to see women wearing traditional Islamic hijab around the campus. This church is located just up the hill from World Relief Seattle in one of the most culturally diverse communities in the Northwest. People from all over the world have moved into the neighborhood because of their connection to this resettlement agency. Many of them are Muslim. The general assumption would be that Muslim women and men wouldn't feel comfortable moving freely in and around a Christian church. Had the church started with what these people believe, conventional wisdom would have proven true—but they didn't. Instead they started with what these families needed. The Hillside Church, in partnership with World Relief, developed a strategy to meet the needs and make friends of their neighbors. Being comfortable for refugees and immigrants is an oasis. Comfort isn't quite belonging, but it is in the same zip code.

Many of the refugees around the church have come from Afghanistan. Because there was no opportunity before coming to the United States for most women to receive an education, the church began to host a World Relief program called Afghan Women's Sewing Club. This ministry allowed the women to do something comfortable and familiar while learning a new language and culture. A room in the church was equipped with sewing machines and cutting tables. Women wearing hijab found a place of comfort inside the church building. The room soon buzzed with activity and laughter. The women were learning to speak English and to read and write while they completed sewing projects. They were finding a place to belong.

One morning after class, two women approached Pastor Debra, who supports this ministry. They asked if there was somewhere in the building that they could go and light a candle to the Virgin Mary's Son. Debra explained that while there was no place in the building that had candles for lighting, there was a room and a place where people could kneel and pray to the Virgin Mary's Son. She asked if they would like to see it, and they followed her to the sanctuary. In the quiet sanctuary Debra gave the women some space to kneel and a place to pray. Afghan women wearing head scarves knelt in a quiet Christian sanctuary to pray to Jesus because they belonged before they believed.[§]

§ Gustavo: During my years serving at the head office for World Relief in Baltimore, Maryland, during the early 2000s, I had the privilege of visiting our office in Seattle. From the parachurch perspective, our role was to find congregations that were willing to embrace refugees as part of their witness to the world. Though there were thousands of churches in the area, few churches engaged in such a welcoming ministry as Hillside. It is a blessing to see that the church in Kent is one such example of a church where everyone belongs.

In an individual story, Randy worked as the onsite foreman for the company that had contracted to complete the expansion project for our church. One part of the plan was the development of a large music room that our music worship pastor had been dreaming about. It wasn't uncommon to see Pastor Ron in conversation with Randy, trying to ensure that his dream for the music room and the finished product matched. It wasn't long before Ron discovered that Randy also had a passion for music. Randy had been playing drums for rock bands in our community since he was in high school. On most weekends he played in bars until the early hours of the morning. Those conversations led to an invitation, and Randy started playing drums with our music team at our two Sunday morning worship services. He would be out until one or two in the morning playing in bars and then up and at the church by eight o'clock on Sunday morning to be ready for the nine o'clock service.

I still remember the first Sunday Randy and Judy joined us for worship. Judy sat toward the back and, as Randy played, kept busily wiping her tears away. Randy had been around church as a kid, and Judy had a Lutheran background. They had tried church once before, but when they had followed people forward to receive Communion the pastor pulled the tray away as Randy reached for the bread. It was a closed Communion for members only: believe, then belong. Randy and Judy never went back.

Randy kept it up for a few months, finishing his set at the bar in the wee hours of the morning, grabbing a nap, and then getting to church early to be ready for worship. One Sunday morning as we were leaving the sanctuary, Randy asked if we could talk. He said he and Judy were really enjoying church and that Judy didn't want to be out late on Saturday night anymore. She was planning to stop going to the bars with the band. He asked me what I thought he should do. I told him I was sure he could trust the Lord to lead him if he asked and that he'd know. A week or so later, Randy let me know that after years of playing with bands in bars, he thought the Lord wanted him to use his skills for worship, and he'd quit the band. One Sunday morning about a year later I baptized Randy. His face was radiant as he came up out of the water. I'm thankful we serve an open Communion, and in more places than just at the Eucharist Table—belonging before believing.∫

> ∫ Stephanie: Thanks be to God for the open Table. The prevenient grace of God—the grace that goes before—comes to us in the bread and the cup. Let those who are thirsty come, even when they don't fully understand their thirst.

The concept of acceptance by the church community as a first step in the faith journey is not innovative. Belonging before believing was at the heart of the seeker-sensitive edge of the church-growth movement of the 1990s and early 2000s. There are numerous examples of churches that have experienced exponential growth by creating church with a come-as-you-are approach. It would be true that most of these churches would never have stated that drawing a crowd was the goal. Even though belonging is the bridge used to lead people to a place of believing, becoming, and a different way of behaving, it can never be the destination. After successfully drawing a crowd to their churches and events, many who attend are stuck on the bridge, identifying with a church but believing and behaving no differently than the culture. Drawing a crowd is intoxicating and can easily create a mission shift from the transformation of lives to the expansion of the influence of a local ministry or pastor. When the mission of the church stops being about changed lives and is focused instead on the success of the organization, we must admit we are stuck on the bridge.

Sometimes the motivation for inclusion first is not driven by evangelism but by a social, philosophical, or even political agenda. Some mainline denominations that have developed a belong-first strategy have abandoned orthodox positions of behavior and belief, desiring to include people who have been disconnected from the church but making belonging their only goal instead of simply their first goal. While churches focused on belonging as the first step of a strategic plan designed for transformational evangelism can get stuck on the bridge of "come as you are," some of these churches seem content with "you belong just as you are." In both cases, the bridge that was intended to lead people not just to a connection with the church but also to a life of devotion to Christ are gridlocked on the on-ramp.

Those who hold the opinion that the first steps to life with Christ are through the door marked Belief worry that the church will pour its resources and energy into methods that don't ultimately result in personal transformation. My first eighteen years as a pastor were spent in ministry to youth. The subject of the correct focus for our ministry was an often-debated topic. Parents of youth who saw the aim of the church as protection of their children from the culture wanted the ministry to focus on behaving and believing. They argued that, if the focus of the ministry to youth was outreach-oriented and successful, the result would be a negative influence on their children. The teens we hoped to draw brought with them experience and perspectives that were not consistent with the hopes and dreams of the parents who were already part of the church. They counted on the church to help maintain their fences. This is a legitimate concern. If the primary interest of the church is the protection of orthodox theology and conformity to a standard of behavior, then encouraging belonging before believing *is* a risky proposition. They wanted the church to play it safe.

When we see the primary responsibility of the church as protection of orthodox belief and adherence to a set of standards, we build fences and walls to keep threatening influences out. After all, Jesus did say, "But small is the gate and narrow the road that leads to life, and only a few find it" (Matthew 7:14). Ironically, though, Jesus also said, "Then the master told his servant, 'Go out to the roads and country lanes and compel them to come in, so that my house will be full'" (Luke 14:23). At first glance these two statements seem contradictory—but not so much when we examine them more closely. Jesus always kept the invitation broad and the transformational terms real. This is the constant tension we must acknowledge if we hope to navigate the wind and waves coming our way without losing our course and missing our destination. Unfortunately, we usually drift one way or the other. Overemphasize belonging, and the substance of the Christian message can be lost in a desire to be open and accepting, taking people as they are with no expectation of change. But overemphasize believing and behaving, and the message of Jesus can be lost in cold, exacting legalism: whatever you're doing isn't good enough; whatever you are considering isn't pure enough. Like Jesus's indictment of the teachers of the law and the Pharisees, we can be guilty of tying heavy, cumbersome loads and putting them on other people's shoulders.

On my way to the office a few years ago, I noticed a building site being prepared for construction. As the framing of the exterior walls began to give shape to the structure, I thought this new building looked like it might be a church. As the project continued, a small steeple at the end of the roof closest to the road confirmed my hunch. It wasn't long before I noticed a man and his wife doing exterior painting and landscaping to prepare the building for a congregation. It turned into a beautiful little chapel, brightly painted with flowers and shrubbery planted, ready for a grand opening. We shouldn't judge people by appearances, but I made some assumptions about the kind of church this little chapel would be by the attire of the

∫ *Stephanie: I question an approach of conditional belonging. If we say a person belongs but only if they agree to change their behavior within a timeframe we deem appropriate, we have reduced belonging to spiritual manipulation.*

couple preparing the building. When the well-crafted sign reading "Holiness Chapel" went up in the side yard, I was pretty sure of the message I would find on the inside.

The couple's choice of clothing and the name of the church were stereotypes of a style of Christianity I am familiar with—one that lends itself to a precise orthodoxy and a rigorous standard of behavior. They made a significant investment of resources to construct the building, and I have no doubt the entire enterprise was a matter of prayer and, likely, fasting. They opened their doors and waited for people to come to the chapel through a narrow gate. Knowing our community and what I assumed was their approach for congregational development, I wasn't surprised when, in a couple of years, the chapel was sold to a preschool and daycare center.

Did the people who planted the church love Jesus? Likely. Did they have a plan for reaching the community with the gospel? It appeared that they did. Was their strategy successful? It wasn't.

On Behaving

If the church is successful at expanding its influence by meeting the felt needs of its neighbors, then an opportunity to share the gospel will naturally follow. At this point, churches are often tempted to stall. After experiencing success bridging the gap between the culture and the Christian community, there is often a struggle.

The tension is that some people can be offended by the claims of the gospel. To avoid the friction and wrestling with this issue, some choose to stay on a needs-meeting mission instead of moving to the gospel.

As an overseer for churches in western Washington, I've had a number of conversations with pastors who have found a connection with their neighbors by offering building space for meetings or volunteering in an area where help was needed and then feeling reluctant to connect the bridge to Jesus. A good example is a church in the city where it would have been difficult to decide whether our church buildings or the congregation itself were in the greatest need of attention. A young, highly effective urban missionary shouldered the responsibility of rebuilding the church along with its reputation in the city. He has been effective at repairing our valuable property and connecting with his neighbors by using the building as a gift to the community. Our image has gone from being a liability and drain on property values to a sought-out venue for neighborhood gatherings. Our pastor's footprint is all over the community, and word on the street is that he can be trusted as a neighbor whose involvement makes things work. The belonging bridge is in place, and the traffic is moving both directions. He is a great example of someone who has allowed his life to be the sermon in a highly secular community where church-planting has been difficult.

As the church tries to build on its positive reputation and establish a worshiping Christian community, the concern is that good friendships can be harmed by what could appear to be a hidden agenda. "I thought we were friends, but now I see you are selling something." Especially when trying to pastor in a city where high-profile religious leaders' failures have been widely publicized, people have suspicions about the motives of organized religion. Sending mixed messages is a legitimate concern, but our desire to be accepted must not detour us from our primary reason to be a presence in the community. Dr. Tom Nees, who found great success in our nation's capital creating safe places for people to belong and meeting their real needs, wisely said that "compassion without evangelism is a cut flower." Carefully and prayerfully, our urban missionary is sharing the love of Jesus and partnering with a church planter to see that all the scattered seed and watering result in a harvest.

The gospel, when it takes root, will always result in changed behavior. There are subtle reasons why belonging before behaving is important. In places where the church leads with behaving, the result can be the idea that we *earn* God's approval and acceptance in the Christian community by our performance. This misrepresentation of the gospel often develops a critical edge to the church and a sense of inadequacy or arrogance in the individual. Change in behavior that brings life is change that happens in response to God's love for us. "We love because he first loved us" (1 John 4:19). While churches may establish codes of character and conduct as guiding principles for believers, they must never be viewed as merits earned for salvation.

Salvation, the gift of God, is worthy of our surrender to his will out of a gratefully obedient heart. "For Christ's love compels us" (2 Corinthians 5:14).

If the gospel we are compelled to share is a list of propositions to accept, an argument to be won, or an organization to join, then leading with believing and behaving would be the right strategy. With this agenda, the importance of establishing a relationship with someone is so it can be the bridge to an opportunity to make a gospel presentation. Packaged evangelism training has often taught techniques for redirecting conversations toward a rehearsed plan of salvation. Recent research makes it clear that few are open to a spiritual conversation that is intentionally propositional. We all know what it feels like to discover during what we thought was a friendly, casual conversation that the other person had a hidden agenda and that we were being led toward a sales pitch or business opportunity. If we don't like this approach in financial matters, why would we assume it would be effective in spiritual matters?

The message of the Gospels reveals that, when God wanted to make his persuasive case with us, he did it incarnationally, not propositionally. As John said in his Gospel according to some translators, "He pitched his tent and lived among us" (see various commentary on 1:14). When we follow the pattern that Jesus used, we find ways to create space for relationships that connect with people where they live and in ways they can understand. Jesus didn't set up a regional office in Nazareth and take appointments—he was always on the move because he came to "seek and to save the lost" (Luke 19:10).

Through a thoughtful congregational evaluation of the overall health of the church where I served as lead pastor, we recognized that need-meeting evangelism was not one of our strengths, and we determined to address it. The congregation had shown significant growth over the years, but most of it was transfer growth. We weren't effective at engaging with people who were not already looking for a place to worship. Rather than trying to devise a way to attract people to what we were already doing, we decided to try something radically different: what if we planted a new church?

The research seemed to indicate that new churches were one of the most effective ways to reach people who were not already connected to a church. What if, instead of going to the expense of leasing new space across town or in a neighboring community, we planted a new work across the parking lot from our sanctuary in our own gym? We wouldn't have all the expenses of a new location; we would just try to reach a different part of our community. We hired a planting pastor and gave him the responsibility of creating a core team to launch a new church focused on people who were unlikely to be drawn to our existing services. We began looking for opportunities to connect outside the walls of our sanctuary. Here is where the story takes a hard left turn. Sometimes the answer is right in front of you. The owner of the local

NASCAR short track regularly attended our second morning worship service, and most of the drivers at the races on Saturday night were not up for church on Sunday morning. The drivers, their families, and many of the fans were people in our community with little or no connection to a church and likely no real interest in church. What could happen if *we* took a real interest in *them*?

Because we were already connected to the owner, there were several ways for our pastor and core team to make connections on a Saturday night at the track. Our music worship team sang the national anthem, our core team developed relationships with drivers and their families, and some of our shade-tree mechanics became part of the pit crew. One of the drivers became part of our core team and opened the way for authentic friendship to be established. Our church plant sponsored him, and the new church's logo covered both sides of his car. He and his family became the first ones to connect with our church, but many more would follow his lead.

Our planting pastor decided to launch the new church on Sunday nights at six o'clock. The new friends we were making would be unlikely to show up on Sunday morning, we knew they (not to mention many others in the community) tended to be busy on Saturday nights, and there were almost no conflicts on Sunday evenings. Our church was already active on Sunday morning, but with exception of a casual evening service in the sanctuary that drew mostly senior adults, the campus was empty on Sunday nights. To be honest, I had my doubts about whether our new NASCAR friends would come, but through the efforts of the core team and the support of the track's owner, they did. Families who would never have connected to one of our morning services became regular attenders on Sunday night. Because it was new, and because bridges of friendship had been built on Saturday nights, they already belonged by the time they came through the doors of our gym. It wasn't long before we were filling the portable swimming pool we'd purchased, and baptism became a regular part of that outreach. I still smile when I remember one Sunday evening when a young mom was baptized and brought her children into the pool with her. Her baptism turned into a sort of pool party as her children had a difficult time grasping the sacred occasion and splashed a bit more than might be considered appropriate—and all of heaven rejoiced![§]

§ Gustavo: This part of the story reminds me of the meeting between Philip and the Ethiopian eunuch on the desert road to Gaza in Acts 8. When the man asked Philip, "What can stand in the way of my being baptized?" Philip didn't send him back to Jerusalem to wait for the proper protocols and schedule to allow the man to be baptized. Baptism, in its purest form, is the sacrament that signifies participation, by faith, in the death and resurrection of Jesus Christ, and the believer's incorporation into his body, the church.

This church-within-a-church was active during the last six of the seventeen years that I served as lead pastor. The pastor who followed me made some changes to the schedule and took the Sunday evening outreach in a different direction. I wondered whether there was any fruit that had lasted for all the effort we had gone to during my tenure. The last time I was with the pastor who succeeded me, I asked him. He said yes, told me one of the drivers and his wife were leading a small group.

Belonging, before behaving, before believing.

On Believing

In the middle of complex circumstances that require us to make a choice, it is not uncommon to hear the familiar phrase "it's hard to know what to believe." *Seeing is believing* was once the gold standard for truth. "I saw it with my own eyes" was all the proof needed in a previous generation. Wasn't that all Thomas said he needed to believe the unbelievable story the other disciples were sharing on resurrection Sunday? Have you noticed that almost no one says, "Seeing is believing" much anymore? There is way too much sleight of hand in our world now to be able to trust our eyes. Just for the fun of it, we had an illusionist come to our annual pastor's retreat. I watched his hands closely, and I still don't know how he made things appear and disappear right before my eyes. I knew there was a trick to it, but seeing wasn't believing—that's what was fun about it. We can alter reality. If Uncle Jacob didn't make it for the family reunion, we can just photoshop him into the picture. There he is, standing next to Aunt Janice in the reunion photo, and soon no one will remember that he stayed home to watch football.

Manipulating what we see and hear to create the illusion of truth happens to us every day—likely hundreds of times a day. Sometimes the manipulation happens to entertain us. Even though the special effects in the movie seem real, we know that what we're seeing is computer-generated and/or happening in front of a green screen. Often the manipula-

WHAT DOES BELONGING BEFORE BELIEVING LOOK LIKE?

tion happens to influence or take advantage of us. If you receive a phone call from a number you don't recognize and the voice on the other end is making fantastic promises or coercive threats, you can be sure someone is trying to deceive you. We are all too aware of unjust prison sentences based on eyewitness accounts, computer-generated images and voices that look and sound like the real thing, news stories that twist the facts, and a constant barrage of calls, tweets, and emails pitching something to accept or purchase. It's no wonder we don't know what to believe anymore! There are logical reasons we find ourselves living among so many skeptics and cynics, and we often find ourselves being drawn in their direction.

∫ Stephanie: What great hope—that belief might begin with doubt! Do our churches have space for such a journey? Or are we too threatened by the questions raised to allow such a disruptive process?

As counterintuitive as it may seem, belief often begins with doubt.∫ The thing about Thomas on resurrection Sunday was that he doubted *because* he wanted to believe. Saul of Tarsus, on the other hand, doubted because he did not want to believe that the carpenter from Nazareth was anything but a fraud. He had a vested interest in the status quo, and Jesus was a direct threat to the system that represented his position of power and privilege. Beyond that, Saul was well educated and could not imagine that Jesus could possibly be the long-awaited Messiah. His death on a Roman cross had proven that rumors of resurrection were simply that. Thomas doubted because he *wanted* to believe—he just didn't want to believe something that wasn't true. He wasn't there, he hadn't seen or heard Jesus's pronouncement of peace over his friends. Secondhand peace would not satisfy his need to know for himself, from his own experience, with his own eyes and ears.

The stories of Saul and Thomas remind us that skepticism and doubt are not the invention of our current post-Christian culture. Questions about what is true will always be part of any real journey that ends in faith. How do we who believe best share the message of Jesus with our increasingly suspicious and cynical neighbors? For some, faith may begin at the end of a propositional argument, but that has never been the path most people travel to faith in Christ. For both Saul and Thomas, the journey required an encounter with the risen Lord.

As the pastor of a local church, four or five times a year I conducted membership classes for people who were interested in our church. At the conclusion of these classes people who attended often decided to become official members. They agreed with our doctrine, embraced the direction of our ministry, understood our denominational connection, and publicly committed themselves to the fellowship of our church. What I found baffling was that far too often people easily agreed to a list of doctrinal statements, joined the church, and then within a short time disappeared from the fellowship. Our membership process was mostly informational and propositional in presentation. We did talk about an experience of salvation and the importance of a daily walk with the Lord, but the class was mostly about what we believed and how we were structured. I think this

§ Gustavo: I have observed that, in places where the church is in the middle of God's movement, the number of members is often smaller than the number of those attending and being active participants in the regular means of worship and fellowship. This means people are interested in what is going on with God's movement in a given location, and they want to be part of it, even though fewer people make the choice to join the specific family (membership). In largely stagnant and over-structured church environments, on the other hand, the number of members tends to exceed the number of active participants because, in many cases, membership gives people the right to belong, which they treat as a graduation stage, even if they are no longer part of the spirit of the movement that they joined in the first place.

emphasis on believing was an important step for people wanting to join our church, but it didn't seem to be the factor that caused them to stay. As a district superintendent, I've observed this same pattern in many of our churches—membership rolls that far exceed the number of active participants. I have reached the conclusion that it is not the believing of similar doctrine that holds the local church together. Rather, belonging is the glue.§

I'm sometimes troubled by the fact that we have so little of the actual teaching of Jesus. Certainly, the Sermon on the Mount is enough to keep us challenged and occupied for the rest of our lives. But, for the most part, the Gospels are filled with Jesus going about doing good, with the disciples close by watching in wide-eyed wonder. There are passages of Scripture where I am left longing for a lot more than the text offers. When Luke tells us that, on the road to Emmaus, "beginning with Moses and all the Prophets, he explained to them what was said in all the Scriptures concerning himself" (24:27), am I the only one who feels like Luke leaves us hanging? It appears to me that Jesus systematically teaches Christology to an audience of two. If there was room on the road for four, I would really have liked to be included. It seems like this would have been a perfect place for a few thousand words of theological instruction. Clearly, however, *what* to believe isn't the focus of the narrative. The story is too busy telling us about the who to give us the details of the what. If forced to choose, would you rather see a sunrise or have a scientific explanation for why some mornings begin with such beautiful colors? It was recognizing him in the breaking of the bread that caused them to go running into the night back to Jerusalem.

It was an encounter with the risen Jesus that transformed Saul's skepticism and eliminated Thomas's doubt. Thomas wasn't there when Jesus first appeared to the disciples on Sunday evening, and we don't know if he was there when the two from Emmaus came bursting through the door. What we do know is that neither testimonies of the disciples' experience nor the Emmaus encounter seemed to resolve Thomas's uncertainty. I can't be sure it happened, but during the week between the first appearance of Jesus and the one that followed where Thomas was present, I can imagine all of the eyewitnesses must have tried to convince Thomas further of the truth of their claims. Surely the two from the Emmaus road took Thomas to Starbucks and had an impromptu apologetics class, right? After all, they had a master's degree in Christology now—having been instructed by the Master.

But when Thomas finds himself in the presence of Jesus, he doesn't say, "Oh, never mind, I'm good—these guys explained it to me!" Believing is complicated, and faith is always somewhat subjective and personal. Doubt is not always a willful choice, and many times it has a benefit. We may believe we can overwhelm someone's doubt or skepticism with persuasive argument, but that is not the way faith is formed for most people. It always gives me pause when I read in Matthew 28 that "the eleven disciples went to Galilee, to the mountain where Jesus has told them to go. When they saw him, they worshiped him; but some doubted" (vv. 16–17). Wait—what? I guess I want a show of hands and an explanation! The text doesn't tell us who it was with doubts this time, but it seems a beautiful thing to me that doubt and obedience are not mutually exclusive.

While Thomas's inclination is to believe and he is surrounded by faith-filled friends, Saul is a hard-core cynic who is full of self-righteousness and "breathing out murderous threats" (Acts 9:1). For both men, their conversion happens on the backside of a miraculous meeting with the resurrected Jesus. While each of their encounters is supernatural, Saul's experience is significantly more dramatic. Thomas heard "peace be with you" (John 20:26). Saul was knocked off his feet by a bright light and heard a voice say, "Saul, Saul, why do you persecute me?" (Acts 9:4). As Saul sat blind for three days trying to sort out what had happened and what it meant for him, provision was already being made for him to belong. Ananias was the bridge used by God to connect him to the faith he had rejected and the mission that would define him.

I've chosen these examples because they represent, in general, the kind of people we encounter when we try to do what Jesus asks us to do—make disciples in the world. On one end of the continuum are people like Thomas, who are drawn to faith but have honest questions about what is true. On the other end are those like Saul, whose attitudes and opinions are fixed and their unbelief deliberate, unwavering, even militant. The reason to assert that belonging precedes believing is that it is rare for someone to come to faith outside of an influential relationship. Even in the dramatic story of the conversion of Paul, it would be a mistake to downplay Ananias's role.

I was complaining to a friend that part of my adjudicatory responsibility required me to be a gatekeeper. He challenged me, "Why don't you be the gate opener instead?"

Gustavo

Jerry's friend asked a good question. If the church is for everyone and if everyone belongs to the fellowship of the seekers and the followers, where is the gate and what is the role of the gatekeepers? And, more poignantly, who are the gatekeepers?

Regardless of the role we play in our formal ministry within our church family, the question of gatekeeping has been a critical one for all three of us, just like it has been for many leaders of local congregations or judicatories. The reality is that pastors and leaders are thrust into the role of local elders or judicatory bishops as part of the institutional church, and by definition they are assigned an overseeing role by the church (in all of their expressions). Whether fulfilling the role of the local overseer (elder) or judicatory overseer (bishop), the New Testament church already had a standard model for governing. The book of Acts indicates that every time the apostles planted a new church, they appointed elders (11:30; 14:23; 15:2; 20:17), and Paul did the same when he turned the church over to local overseers (1 Timothy 3:1–7; Titus 1:5). By the second century, however, the governance structure of the church had turned these facilitators of orthodoxy and orthopraxy into the gatekeepers of the church—a role that accelerated the paradigmatic shift away from the original model established by Jesus and closer to the same rigid model that the Pharisees had before Jesus came—hence the importance of Jerry's friend's question.

In looking at his declaration to the Pharisees in John 10, we can see Jesus make a distinction between the sheep and the gate and, very particularly, the role of the gatekeeper. In the metaphor that Jesus introduced to the Pharisees, who saw themselves as gatekeepers, Jesus paradoxically introduces himself as shepherd, gate, *and* gatekeeper—an interesting metaphor that confused those who wanted to define who was in and who was out on the basis of rules and behaviors only. First, Jesus declares that he is the gate, the only way to the fold. Then Jesus declares that he is the good shepherd, the one who lays down his life for his own sheep. But his overall declaration is that he is the only one who chooses and calls all the sheep to the fold. He is the gatekeeper—the way to the Father.

So if Jesus is the gate and the shepherd *and* the gatekeeper, what are we—those of us thrust into the eldership and oversight of the church? If we assume we are gatekeepers, we will quickly enter into the same behaviors of the well-intended Pharisees and the well-intended early fathers and mothers of the church, and we will become the ones who determine who belongs and who doesn't. Perhaps, instead, we should consider ourselves as only groundskeepers?

Stephanie

How does belong-before-believe start? We begin by humbling ourselves before God and others. It is easy to forget that we too have been delivered from a life of sin. Perhaps our journey took a different shape, but we are no less in need of God's grace. We remember we are not the source of salvation or transformation. We are not the Redeemer. We are the redeemed. As Gustavo has already quoted, we are beggars who tell others where we have found bread. When we release ourselves from the idolatrous role of being god in the life of another, we—and those around us—experience freedom.

Having humbled ourselves and living in the blessed reminder that we are not in fact God, we suspend judgment. We have opinions and convictions—and rightly so. However, how often does a person come to know and love Jesus because we highlight all the ways in which we believe they are falling short? Rarely. Our judgment is not redemptive; it wounds and shames. If we can suspend judgment, take a pause in imposing ourselves and our views on another, we might have the privilege of seeing the Spirit move in unexpected ways. May we never become a stumbling block to someone who is hungering after God.

Once we have surrendered ourselves fully and entrusted others to the Spirit, we are able to actively welcome. No longer bound by pride or judgment, we are joyfully free to serve and connect. We eagerly search for ways that our lives can intentionally intersect with those in search of belonging and transformation. We open our lives to others in hope and love. We might just have the privilege of bearing witness to life transformation as we create space for others to belong if we simply live faithfully before them.

5. BELONGING TO THE WAY, BELIEVING IN THE TRUTH, EXPERIENCING LIFE

Gustavo

Whether you turn to the right or to the left,
your ears will hear a voice behind you,
saying, "This is the way; walk in it."
—Isaiah 30:21

My wife, Rachel, and I moved with our family to an American suburb because of my ministry assignment when our daughters were still at home. Our home was in a cul-de-sac where we got to know all our neighbors and our daughters could play with their kids. Tammy was one of our neighbors. She was a divorced mom, living at home with her only child and in a codependent relationship with an abusive partner.

Rachel has been the evangelist of the family. She rarely preaches or teaches from a pulpit or lectern, but she has always been an evangelist. In every neighborhood where we have lived—and there have been at least a dozen because of our missionary ministry—Rachel's natural evangelistic friendship has manifested itself to bless our neighbors. Tammy was no exception. I must confess I was not fond of Tammy. She seemed to be always in a hurry, yelling at her kid and her partner, and the only time I saw her smile was when she came to our doorstep to offer cosmetics that she sold using a pyramid scheme—something I've never had much taste for because I thought it manipulated the goodwill of neighbors and friends.

Fortunately, none of this was an issue for Rachel. As her natural self, Rachel engaged Tammy, opening her heart and our home for Tammy to come and promote the products she sold. Over time, Tammy opened up to Rachel, and, though I don't know much about what they discussed, I know that Tammy saw Rachel as more than merely a neighbor or a customer.

After several such visits, knowing we were "church folk," Tammy asked Rachel if she could host an event at our home with "church ladies." By then we knew Tammy did not have the best opinion of church because her former husband was a Catholic man who had been faithful to the traditions of the church but had made her and her son's lives miserable. I often overheard Tammy referring to church and church people in demeaning ways, so I was surprised to hear she wanted to host a sales presentation in our home with church ladies. *Then again*, I thought, *this is what a pyramid scheme does. It takes advantage of your networks with an eye toward the bottom line.* (I know what you may be thinking—and yes, I ate my humble pie!)

In reality, the sales presentation was only an excuse—it was Jesus's excuse to start working on Tammy's heart. First, thanks to the sales presentation—and the subsequent visits to our home and the homes of the other ladies at church—Tammy started asking questions about Jesus. She had been exposed to the concept of Jesus at the beginning of her failed marriage, but she had given up trying to know him. For her, Jesus was a distant image, the head of a religion many people followed but whom few of them seemed to know, and even fewer represented him well. But Jesus was already at work in Tammy's life. Through her interactions with Rachel and the church ladies, Tammy started opening up to the possibility that Jesus was more than a theory or a religious construct. She saw that the church ladies were just as human as she was and that they gathered to talk about issues similar to the ones she faced at home and at work. The only difference was that these ladies seemed to be at peace, and they were joyful, patient, and fun. Tammy was intrigued.

Rachel and I decided to begin hosting our small group whenever I was at home, on a rotational basis. As the evangelist in the family, Rachel decided to invite Tammy to our small group gatherings at home. Since she was already intrigued and open to the idea of exploring the journey of the church ladies—we call that prevenient grace—Tammy agreed to join us. She began the journey. She started on the Way.

Our small group had eight families, all with young children, reflecting the typical makeup of a suburban family. There were a couple of multiracial families, a couple of divorced single mothers, a couple of divorcées in their second marriages, working-class and middle-class families, a missionary family, and the pastoral family. There was enough diversity in the group that Tammy felt comfortable being just the way she was.

For months Tammy joined the small group meetings faithfully. She started participating and asking questions about Jesus, church, and faith. At the beginning, her questions were what some church people might consider "off the mark" (by the way, in the journey with Jesus, there *are* no off-the-mark questions—he listens to all with care). We could tell she was thirsty and searching, and the group often detoured from the study guide to tend to Tammy's questions. But that was not enough. Through the interaction with the group we realized that Tammy's life was really a mess—relationally, financially, and in other ways. But the group loved her and her ten-year-old son.

Months passed, and Tammy started attending our church most Sundays. She never missed small group, and she no longer relied on Rachel's friendship to relate to the people at church. At times, she even jokingly referred to herself as a "church lady but still doing some stuff that you ladies don't do.'' Neverthe-less, we all rejoiced to hear her referring to Jesus as more than a theory or religious construct (at best), or as a distant God nobody can talk to. She often asked for prayer for her son and for her relationship.

One day, while Rachel and I were traveling, Rachel got a text that made her yell with excitement. Tammy had been at the church's ladies' retreat. On one of the evenings at the retreat, while they were studying the main purpose of Jesus coming to this earth, Tammy understood the depths of the plan of salvation. She grasped the simplest and deepest truth that Jesus was God and that he was the ladder stretching from heav-en to earth, connecting the holy with the human. She understood that, by eating with sinners and seekers, Jesus had put his love of people ahead of piety and religion. She was thankful our church family had provided a safe place for her hunger and her search, and she had allowed God's prevenient grace to work in her as she journeyed, just the way she was. Now, after journeying with Jesus and Jesus people, she had discovered the truth and accepted it. The text mes-sage was short, but the meaning was eternal: Tammy had embraced Jesus as the only way to salvation—her friend, her savior, and her companion.

As most missionaries do, Rachel and I eventually moved with our family to the next assignment. We said goodbye to the church, the small group, and the neighborhood. We said goodbye to Tammy, who was still walking the journey of grace. Months after we left town and about a year after Tammy's conversion, we saw pictures on Facebook that showed Tammy as part of the music worship team at our former church. We knew she had a gift for music and theater. God had just been waiting for her to turn to him to use her gifts.

By then, God's Spirit had turned Tammy's life around. She ended the abusive relationship she had with her live-in boyfriend and met a man in church who was also a member of the music worship team. A year or so later, they got married, and it has now been nearly two decades since that happened. We don't have much contact with Tammy nowadays, but there are some things we know for sure: God's prevenient grace put us in contact with Tammy so she would enter her journey of faith through a neighbor. Our church provided the table for her hunger to be satisfied without any prejudices or taboos, which allowed Tammy to get to know the truth that set her free. And her life changed, abundantly. What was this journey all about? Was Tammy's journey what Jesus meant when he said, "I am the way and the truth and the life" (John 14:6)?

During the winter of 2011, a friend and I started exploring Jesus's statement to the disciples as recorded in John 14:6: "I am the way and the truth and the life." My friend suggested that, sometimes, the church has looked at this profound statement as a single-truth affirmation only. We have presented this statement as a whole package that we receive when we receive Jesus. And this is true in a practical sense:

- When we receive Jesus as our Lord and Savior, we enter the Way—the only way to salvation. The apostles echoed this claim when they stated that "there is salvation in no one else, for there is no other name under heaven given among mortals by which we must be saved" (Acts 4:12, NRSV) and that "if you declare with your mouth, 'Jesus is Lord,' and believe in your heart that God raised him from the dead, you will be saved" (Romans 10:9).

- When we receive Jesus as our Lord and Savior, we embrace the Truth, who sets us free from guilt, sin, and condemnation. John wrote to the early believers, affirming that "we know also that the Son of God has come and has given us an understanding, so that we may know him who is true. And we are in him who is true by being in his Son Jesus Christ. He is the true God and eternal life" (1 John 5:20).

- When we receive Jesus as our Lord and Savior, we receive the gift of abundant and eternal life. Earlier in the Gospel of John, Jesus told the disciples, "I have come that they may have life, and have it to the full" (10:10b). In fact, there are more references to Christ as Life than affirmations of him as the Way or the Truth. Paul makes reference not only to the gift of abundant life in his writings to the first-century church but also to the change in a person's life thanks to the work of Christ in us: "Therefore, if anyone is in Christ, the new creation has come: The old has gone, the new is here!" (2 Corinthians 5:17).

These three true realities of Jesus being the Way, the Truth, and the Life have been and continue to be some of the bedrocks of the Christian faith. Unfortunately, as true and definite as they are, these three statements, presented as a one-block truth, limit the breadth of the meaning that Jesus wanted to share with the disciples. These three statements can be and have been used as essential in Christian apologetics to affirm the Person of Christ as one of the "I AMs" of Jesus in the Gospel of John in relationship to salvation and eternal life. However, in looking at the stories we have shared in this book, we believe that Christ's statement was broader than a mere apologetic affirmation. This statement described for the disciples and for the church today the journey of grace that he had come to introduce to his creation as we follow him, believe in him, and find everlasting life in him.

∫ Stephanie: We must not underestimate the power of prevenient grace—God working in our lives long before we are aware of it. As followers of Jesus, we are invited to cooperate with this grace by loving and welcoming those who do not yet know Jesus, in order that they might awaken to the grace at work in their lives.

This expanded interpretation of Jesus's declaration helps us understand the journey on which we all travel throughout our lives, and it also helps us understand the idea of belonging before believing and behaving in the life of the church. Tammy didn't embrace the Way, the Truth, and the Life all at once. Thanks to God's prevenient grace, she started becoming familiar with the Way by being in contact with people who belonged to the Way. These were people who loved Jesus and who were used by Jesus to show Tammy the Way. Through his disciples, Jesus prepared Tammy's heart to join his mission and to intersect her journey with his.

I Am the Way, You Belong

For many, to say that Jesus is the Way is simply to present the closing argument to justify our religious beliefs. Some of us use that statement as a categorical way to defend the veracity and authenticity of Christianity as the only way to salvation. There is truth to that, but Jesus meant more when he made this profound revelation. The disciples, with very little theological preparation (and representing the majority of people), struggled with the idea of knowing God—the Father and Creator. Centuries of religion had made them believe that the only way to know God was through the practice of their rituals[∫] and the fulfillment of the law—which, to a great extent, had distanced them from God, who was accessible only through the mediation of the high priests. So when Jesus responded to their question "How can we know the way?" (John 14:5), he was not making a religious statement. What Jesus was saying was "*I am the Way*—follow it. Follow *me*." His statement was an invitation to journey with him, to learn from him, and to witness the incarnation of the Father among us in truth and grace (see John 1:14).

In making the statement, "I am the way," Jesus was presenting two equally essential realities that are not mutually exclusive. First, he was making the eternal

> ∫ Stephanie: It's an oversimplification of the issue to dismiss the disciples (and Israel before them) as legalistic. At the heart of the issue was a loss of their identity as the people of God. Jesus came proclaiming the kingdom of God, a kingdom in which Israel was called to be a light to the nations. Israel had forgotten their vocation, however, particularly as it related to the marginalized and outsiders. Instead, they had focused on the privilege that came with being the chosen people of God. The idea that their long-awaited Messiah was the poor son of a carpenter who insisted on giving himself freely to the least of these was not just unpalatable—it was offensive! No wonder the leaders of the day had no interest in following this Messiah.

∫ *Stephanie: It has been my experience that the statement "I am the way" has been treated less as a call to walk in the way of Jesus and more as theological ammunition against those outside the Christian faith. It is an evangelistic nonstarter, however, since those who do not know Jesus also do not affirm the Bible as the authoritative Word of God. Therefore, it only serves to entrench those who question the veracity of Jesus's claim. Instead, perhaps we ought to direct our energy toward walking the way of Jesus faithfully, which will naturally lead us to creating authentic spaces for belonging.*

statement that there is no other path to heaven to be *with* the Father. This was a salvific statement. The exclusive nature of the only route to salvation for all humanity is affirmed in the words "I am the way."∫ Peter understood, embraced, and preached the depth of this statement after the Pentecost when he told the religious leaders that "there is salvation in no one else, for there is no other name under heaven given among mortals by which we must be saved" (Acts 4:12, NRSV).

At the same time, Jesus was reminding the disciples that he was the only way to get to *know* God the Father. The first Christians were so convinced that Jesus was the only way to know God that they taught this truth everywhere they went and were called "followers of the Way" (see Acts 24:14). Entering the Way meant that, as followers of Jesus, we were to go beyond studying who Jesus was and what he did. Followers of the Way were to have an intimate relationship with Jesus, which would allow them to open their hearts and lives and, in the process, discover the great revelation of the Word who became flesh and allowed them to see his full glory in truth and grace.

Even though Jesus knew he was the Way, he did not play favorites in allowing people to be his followers. His invitation was open. His call was simple. His requirements were minimal. "Follow me," he said. "I am the gate—enter through me. Come to me, all you who are weary and burdened." This was Tammy's story. This was my story. This was the story of many.

I Am the Truth, You Believe

The beauty of journeying with Jesus is that, once we establish a personal, loving, intimate relationship with him and him alone, we allow the Spirit of God to continue his work of prevenient grace to the point that we discover, by grace, that he is indeed the only way to save us from our past and present of sin and guilt. This moves the marker in our lives. We move from journeying with Jesus and living with him to allowing Jesus to come into our lives to live in us. This is the truth of the gospel. Through following Jesus and journeying with him, we don't just gain new insight about living and relating to the world (which is central to his teachings). When we discover, through the convicting work of the Holy Spirit, that he is the Truth and we embrace that truth, we are given the gift of abundant and eternal life. We recognize this as God's saving grace for us.

Being a follower who has entered the Way is not enough. Throughout the course of the journey, followers of Jesus have an encounter with the truth that reveals not only who Jesus is but also who we are without him. And our attitude toward that truth determines the course of our lives. If we accept the truth and embrace it, we are freed from guilt and sin: "And you will know the truth, and the truth will make you free" (John 8:32, NRSV). Conversely, if we don't love the truth, we resist salvation. Believing is the natural next step in the journey of grace. Embracing God's saving grace is a natural outcome of walking in the Way: "The first step on the way of truth is taken when Jesus shines his light into our lives and we acknowledge that we are sinners in need of forgiveness, atonement, and justification. This causes us to repent."[11]

Yet, just as we have seen even in this book, not everyone who belonged to the fellowship of Jesus's followers continued on the journey with him. Many followed and entered the journey. Very few believed. In fact, Jesus spoke about this reality when he made a distinction between the broad and the narrow way as a process of willful self-selection in response to God's prevenient grace (see Matthew 7:13–14). Although we affirm that "the grace of God through Jesus Christ is freely bestowed upon all people, enabling all who will to turn from sin to righteousness, believe on Jesus Christ for pardon and cleansing from sin, and follow good works pleasing and acceptable in his sight," we also confess that "the human race's creation in Godlikeness included the ability to choose between right and wrong, and that thus human beings were made morally responsible" for their choice to believe or not.[12]

That's the difference between Tammy's story and Richard's story. Richard was a young man who at-

∫ *Stephanie: This is the Wesleyan tension of responsible grace. God is the faithful initiator; we are responders as the Holy Spirit empowers us. Our work is always secondary to the primary work of God. Not even an act of the will precedes the invitation of God.*

11. "What Did Jesus Mean When He Said That He Was the Truth?" *Active Christianity*, n.d., https://activechristianity.org/what-did-jesus-mean-when-he-said-that-he-was-the-truth.
12. Church of the Nazarene, *Manual: 2017–2021*, "VII. Prevenient Grace" (Kansas City, MO: Nazarene Publishing House, 2017), 29.

tended my youth group when I was the group leader. He had come from a difficult past of drugs, alcohol, and promiscuity when he joined our youth group in Guatemala. For months, Richard was the trouble-maker in the group until one day I invited him to spend some time at my parents' home. We embraced him and loved him and, like Tammy, he joined our group and became an active member of the youth. His charismatic personality allowed Richard to be a leader in the youth group, and he became quickly accepted by church members, old and young alike. He changed from being erratic and undecided about his future to becoming a successful college graduate and professor. Even though Richard belonged to the Way and studied about Jesus—and even claimed to be one of his followers—Richard never fully embraced the truth. Even to this day, he resists salvation. We still love Richard and often talk to him and remind him of the truth, which we hope he will one day embrace.

I Am the Life, You Become Like Me

The anchor of Jesus's statement in John 14:6 was his revelation that he is the Life. The ultimate purpose of God's incarnation in the person of Jesus and the ultimate purpose of Jesus's death on the cross was not for us to follow him but for us to find life in him. The Gospel of John encapsulates the purpose of Jesus's mission of reconciliation and salvation: "For God so loved the world [everyone belongs] that he gave his one and only Son, that whoever [not everyone but *whoever*] believes in him shall not perish but have eternal life" (3:16).

The main reason for a follower to become a believer is not so the believer will become part of a religious group or even the broader church of Jesus Christ. Jesus told the disciples he had come so we would enjoy life, and life to the fullest. "Through our relationship with Jesus, the Father, Son, and Holy Spirit, we receive the gift of life. Because Jesus *is* the Life."[13] It seems as if Jesus is emphasizing that, just as he is the Way, and everyone is welcome to join the Way, we will embrace the Truth that sets us free, and then, and only then, will we find Life.

Abundant life—life in its fullness—can only happen through the work of the Holy Spirit. When Jesus said he had come so that we may enjoy fullness of life, he meant all areas of our life. He referred to the work of his Holy Spirit to continue the perfecting work in us as we journey with him. Paul accentuated that promise of God's sanctifying grace: "May God himself, the God of peace, sanctify you through and through. May your whole spirit, soul and body be kept blameless at the coming of our Lord Jesus Christ. The one who calls you is faithful, and he will do it" (1 Thessalonians 5:23–24). This doxology serves also as the capstone for Jesus's statement. He who calls (the Way) will keep us blameless as we declare him as our Lord

> ∫ Stephanie: To focus our attention exclusively on abundant life, now and into eternity, without deeply engaging our vocation to serve the world is a misunderstanding of the gospel. Abundant life that does not nourish the world is not abundant life. It is selfishness dressed up in its Sunday best. Like Abraham, we are blessed to be a blessing—not merely to experience abundant, joyful living now and forever.

13. Glen Burris, "I Am the Way, the Truth, and the Life," in Sweet and Davis, *We Are the Church*, 217.

(the Truth), and he will sanctify all areas of our life both now and forever (the Life).

Leonard Sweet and Frank Viola summarize the focus of Jesus's mission as a life-giving mission: "Each sign in John's Gospel set forth what life in the kingdom of God practically means. To put it another way, they reveal the nature of eternal life—a life that has been given to us now in Jesus Christ. Jesus Christ as eternal life is the central theme of John's Gospel."[14]

Tammy's story is an illustration of the journey of grace that Jesus introduced in his response to the disciples' inquiry. Thanks to God's prevenient grace, Tammy was exposed to the Way, and she chose to follow it. All she needed was a willing church that would introduce her to the Way. She did not need to be introduced to religion or even to faith. All she needed was to be welcomed into the Way. In the process, and thanks to the work of the Holy Spirit in her life, she was able to discern the Truth. She chose to embrace the Truth. She chose to receive the gift of God's saving grace. As she continues her journey, we pray that God's sanctifying grace has taken hold of Tammy's heart and life so that she can enjoy all the dimensions of the life in the kingdom of God availed to her by her journey with Jesus—the Way, the Truth, and the Life.

---

14. Leonard Sweet and Frank Viola, *Jesus: A Theograpy* (Nashville: Thomas Nelson, 2012), 170.

6. BELONGING BEFORE BELIEVING
Just Like the Blind Man

Jerry

When I was a freshman in college, I lived a couple doors down the hall from Michael Benson. Mike had a contagious laugh, and I found it easy to be his friend. I still remember the day Mike dropped by my room with a book in his hand. His father had written it, and he wondered if I would like a copy. It was a gift. "Sure," I said.

Bob Benson's book opened a window for me that I didn't know existed. He talked about God's grace in ways that were compelling and within reach. Growing up I had been taught that God loved us, but that was never more than a concept for me. It seemed pretty clear, from the messages I heard from the evangelists who came through our little church a couple times a year, that God didn't like us much. We all know instinctively that perfect fear casts out love.

I tend to speak softly as a preacher because there is a tone and decibel level that creates frost on my soul.

Bob talked about God in ways I'd never heard before, ways that warmed my soul instead of chilling it. He included a poem in his book about dropping Mike off at college. "Parental Math" beautifully tells the story of a father's love and the pain of separation. The concluding stanzas read:

> And I was thinking about God.
> He sure has plenty of children—
> plenty of artists, plenty of singers
> and carpenters and candlestick makers
> and plenty of everybody except you.
> And all of them together
> can never take your place.
> And there will always be
> an empty chair at his table
> when you're not home.
>
> And if once in a while
> it seems as if he's crowding you a bit—
> try to forgive him.
> It may be one of those nights
> when he misses you so much
> he can hardly stand it.[15]

---

15. Robert Benson, *"See You at the House:" The Very Best of the Stories He Used to Tell* (Nashville: Thomas Nelson, 1989), 63–64.

The idea of an active, pursuing love of God is at the heart of the gospel, and one of the Articles of Faith for my denomination. Prevenient grace—the outward-focused, inclusive love of God—is central to the thesis of this book. We believe that the impulse to *include* is deeply rooted in what it means to be the body of Christ in the world. While the desire to include is divine in origin, the impulse to *exclude* is all too human,∫ revealing how far we have fallen from the *imago Dei*. Voting people from the stage and "off the island" has become an all too familiar hobby that has been exacerbated by social media. It isn't enough to articulate a disagreement in ideology. Total destruction of a real or perceived opponent seems too often to be the agenda. Although technology has changed the method, the impulse is as old as Cain and Abel. We have a tendency to distort the lyrics of the gospel song. Instead of looking beyond their faults and seeing their needs, as Jesus did and still does for us, we tend to look beyond people's needs and see their faults.

John 9 tells a wonderful story of the sudden inclusion of a man who was born blind. I don't know that it is a correct comparison to identify the disciples with church folks, but we do both have the reputation of hanging around Jesus. The disciples' first impulse in this story is to find fault. I'm feeling conviction even as I write this. From the moment they laid eyes on him, the judgment of their hearts came right out of their mouths: "Rabbi, who sinned, this man or his parents, that he was born blind?" (v. 2). *Spoiler alert: everybody in this passage has cataracts.* The assump-

> ∫ Stephanie: The impulse to exclude is not inherently human; it is an expression of our fallen nature. Exclusion is indicative of two things. First, it indicates a belief in the myth of scarcity: there is simply not enough, so I must exclude others to get what is mine. Second, it indicates that I have formed my identity over and against the other: I am not them, thus I am me; I must exclude the other in order to know who I am. To be truly human—the way God created and intended us to be—is to reject the myth of scarcity and trust in the provision of God. To be truly human is to know myself first as a child of God and thereby have nonthreatening space within myself for the other.

tion in first-century Judaism was that, if someone was suffering, they deserved it. The idea that this man had a prenatal sin that deserved a lifetime of blindness seems twisted—and Jesus says so. The disciples have ignored the man's need in favor of jumping to a conclusion and initiating a theological debate.[§] They have already drawn lines of exclusion before they've even engaged, before they have listened to his story.

§ Gustavo: This impulse has not changed. Unfortunately, many segments of the church spend more time debating the theology or sociology of sin instead of realizing that anything that keeps humans away from God's standard of life in its fullness is a good opportunity for the love and work of Christ to be displayed in their lives.

Again, I'm feeling convicted as I write this. Jesus turns the conversation upside down by suggesting that this man's suffering might serve a higher purpose. God's glory is not absent from but is revealed in the midst of suffering. This is good news for the blind man and for us as well. All of the dialogue may not be included in the text, but this appears to be a drive-by healing. There was no "Jesus, son of David, have mercy on me!" plea from the man born blind (see Matthew 9:27; 15:22; 20:30–31; Mark 10:47–48; Luke 18:38–39). There are no friends with faith bringing him for healing (see Matthew 9:2–8; Mark 2:1–12; Luke 5:17–26). Not even the disciples express concern for the blind man's condition. Jesus just reaches into the darkness and brings light to his world—belonging before he even knows what to believe.

Jesus makes a simple request: "Go, wash in the Pool of Siloam" (John 9:7). Although we are not required to initiate our own rescue, we must participate in it. A simple act of obedience often precedes faith. "So the man went and washed, and came home seeing" (v. 7).

Sometimes when I read Scripture, I am intrigued by what gets included. The debate that ensues when the blind man returns seeing is one of those times when I want to speculate a bit. The people who are first to witness the miraculous healing are described as his neighbors. Yet they don't know him well enough to immediately rejoice with him. They may be neighbors, but they aren't friends. They only know him well enough to describe him by his disability and define him by his status—blind beggar. The conversation that ensues among his neighbors is a disagreement about his identity. Is this the man or just his doppelganger?

Listening to the discussion about himself, the man becomes his own identifier, at which point the neighbors demand to know how this could have happened. Someone needs to notify a Pharisee! What, no celebration? Indifference is its own special kind of blindness.∫

With his eyes open and his blindness no longer defining him, the man is not interested in sitting on the sidelines. Jesus has included him in a way that no one ever has. All he knows is that he went and washed, and now he can see. "I don't know" is what he has to say to the rest of their questions. I want to be careful not to try too hard to squeeze this narrative into our belonging-before-believing motif, but "I don't know" is a perfectly acceptable answer for someone exploring the path to faith.§∫ When we make believing a prerequisite to belonging, people often step away or give verbal assent to things they have not internalized.

∫ Stephanie: Indifference is the result of privilege. I am unaffected by an issue; therefore, it is not an issue. Why should I care? Indifference leads us to ignore those who are being excluded because we ourselves are not being excluded. We are numb to our responsibility to actively work for justice and change for those who have been excluded.

§ Gustavo: This is a convicting thought. Sometimes we expect people to become believers when they see the work of God in their lives through healing, deliverance, etc. The blind man did exactly what Jesus told him—to go to the pool and wash—yet the man was not instantly a believer. He was a pragmatic man who was trying to see. How many of us in our pragmatic religion come to Christ only to get healed, financed, or helped, without really believing in him?

∫ *Stephanie: Does God only respond to our need if we believe the right things in the right ways? This story seems to suggest otherwise. The man does not understand, yet Jesus shows him mercy. He does not know who Jesus is or understand his mission, but he persistently tells his story of healing without wavering. His honest wrestling with his experience is rewarded when he becomes witness to one of Jesus's clearest confessions of his messianic identity: "'Do you believe in the Son of Man?' 'Who is he, sir?' the man asked. 'Tell me so that I may believe in him.' Jesus said, 'You have now seen him; in fact, he is the one speaking with you'" (John 9:35–37). We all come to God imperfectly, often selfishly, even opportunistically, but grace is not thwarted by our wayward hearts. God's welcome is not contingent upon our perfect understanding or unsullied motives. God simply says, "Come."*

I want to leave a gracious space for "I don't know." Most people are not interested in being told what to believe but often respond positively to open-ended conversations where their story and our listening become more important than our agenda.

In my job as an overseer, I often find myself on airplanes headed to and from meetings. I've taken to praying, "Lord Jesus, if I can be a source of encouragement to someone next to me on this flight, I would be happy to do it" as I step onto the plane. I have had some wonderful conversations in fuselages. One that stands out for me happened on a flight from Baltimore to Seattle. Because Southwest Airlines has a first-come-first-served approach to seating, the earlier you check in for your flight the better your choice of seats will be when boarding. I always try to check in early enough to be able to get an aisle seat. On this flight, however, I ended up getting on the flight later than I prefer so that, by the time I boarded the plane, all the aisle seats were taken. I squeezed over the knees of a man on the aisle and sat by the window. (At least I wasn't in the middle!)

I turned to the man on the aisle and said, "You probably don't want to get into an intense conversation with me, but it could be to our advantage."

He predictably said, "What?"

I explained that the flight looked like it would be full and that people were unlikely to sit down in the middle of an intense conversation. We could have a good chance of keeping the seat between us empty, giving the two of us a more comfortable flight if we leaned into the middle and spoke passionately with hand gestures.

He said, "I'm in."

I asked why he was headed for Seattle. He worked for the Navy and he was going to check out a couple of ships in Tacoma.

It worked like a charm. Everyone walked right past our row, filling the plane and leaving our middle seat empty. When boarding was nearing completion, a tall, slender young man said, "Excuse me, that's my seat," and pointed to the one between us.

I said, "Who does that—sits down in the middle of an intense conversation?"

"I do," he said. "That is the last seat on the plane, and it's mine." Then he stepped over the knees of my new friend and settled into the middle seat. The two of them chatted for a bit, and then he turned to me and asked, "What do you do?"

This is where the conversation always gets interesting. Some people have had very little direct exposure to a pastor. His initial response when I answered was a bit cold. Recent current events had created stereotypes in his mind that came out in questions that were really more position statements than inquiries. As I fielded his questions, I was careful to help him understand that I did not think it was my job to force everyone to live by my moral and theological code. There were things that were important to me, that I held sacred, but I was not trying to force my agenda on everyone else. He relaxed a bit.

"What do you do?" I asked. He was a statistics professor and was flying to Seattle to teach at the University of Washington for a few days.

"And what do you believe?" I asked him.

"I am an atheist," he said.

My response was, "You can't be."

His mood turned chilly again. "What do you mean?" he snapped.

"Well," I said. "You're a statistics professor. What are the odds that chance plus time equals all the beauty we see around us? I mean, chance plus time equals your wife, music, love, and the complexity of the universe?"

He was quiet for a minute, and I could see that he was calculating in his mind. "I'm an agnostic," he said.

"I really don't think you are," I said. The temperature between us dropped again. "I mean, that is such a pessimistic position! I think as a statistics professor you have to be at the very least a *possibilitist*! It is a much more positive place to live. I mean, it must at

least be *possible* that there is intelligence behind all
that we see and experience."

He was calculating again and didn't respond.

After a moment I asked, "What's your background?"

"I'm Jewish," he said, "and my wife is Hindu, but
neither of us practices any religion."

"You're Jewish?" I said.

"Yes, my grandparents used to attend synagogue, but
my parents didn't, and I never have," he explained.

"Would you like to know your story?" I asked.

"What story is that?"

"You know—Abraham, Isaac, and Jacob." I waited
as he thought about it.

"I think maybe I would," he finally said.

With his permission, I spent the next four hours
telling the story of Israel and God's promise to bless
the world through Abraham. I told him that if he was
a Jew, it was because he was from the tribe of Judah.
Somewhere over the Midwest I said, "I'm sure it
won't surprise you to know that I'm a big fan of Jesus,
and he was Jewish too."

He didn't know that, but quietly said, "I don't have
anything against Jesus."

"I don't think anybody who really knows him does," I said.

As we landed in Seattle, he kindly said, "This is the best conversation I've ever had on an airplane, and I think I *am* a possibilitist."

I am reminded that a sower went out to sow, and the seed fell in many places. When I was picking up my luggage from the carousel at baggage claim, the man from the Navy was picking up his bag and turned to me and said, "I think I'm a possibilitist too."

In John 9, the newly sighted man has a story to tell. His blindness has excluded him from synagogue discussions and Sabbath worship, but he has received his sight and is about to find his voice. It seems absurd that the response of his neighbors is not wonder and joy but instead suspicion. Instead of organizing a block party, they take him to the Pharisees for a legal analysis and a judgment. The teachers of the law conclude this about Jesus: "This man is not from God, for he does not keep the Sabbath" (v. 16). I know you're thinking that's ridiculous, and you're not the only one.

Someone in the crowd raises a hand and asks the obvious question: "How can a sinner perform such signs?" (v. 16).

The frightening thing is that they care more about their understanding of orthodoxy than they do that the man has received his sight. It is no coincidence that Jesus chose to heal this man on the Sabbath. He did it to make exactly that point.

I'm typing very quietly now because I wonder how many times I've been guilty of thinking I was protecting the faith, doing God's work—and missed a miracle. It seems ironic that the man's blindness excludes him from fellowship and then so does his healing. He can't explain it and doesn't understand it, but he knows which team he's on. When they finally ask what he has to say, he finds his voice and declares, "He is a prophet" (v. 17). It's a good answer and a logical assumption. He's already resolved the question about how a sinner could do such miraculous things, but his understanding is limited. I want to be part of a church that leaves a lot of room for people to explore what it means to follow Jesus without having it all figured out. It should give us pause that the people in the story who think they have it all figured out, don't.

John makes it clear that this story revolves around Jesus's statement, "I am the light of the world" (v. 5). In this account, vision for one man becomes a living parable of a greater truth. It is what Jesus means when he says, "This happened so that the works of God might be displayed in him" (v. 3). I wish I knew his name because, as I write about him, I'm not sure what to call him—the man born blind? the newly seeing man? the man formerly known as the man born blind? The truth is that if you don't know someone's name, you don't really have a relationship. I may be reading too much into the text, but it seems telling

> ∫ *Stephanie: It is worth nothing that inclusion by Jesus results in exclusion by the religious establishment. The church would do well to remember that Jesus continually works at the margins. Might God be working most profoundly in and among those we are eager to exclude? What if our exclusion precludes us from bearing witness to God's salvific and transformative action among the least of these?*

that no one calls him by name or seems to care about what has happened for him. They talk about him in front of him as if he isn't there, and only address him directly as a last resort.

This is often what happens when we define people by categories we choose for them. Jesus sees individuals and ignores the labels. That's why he is frequently in trouble for where he goes and whom he eats with. Light enters this man's life for the first time, and everything begins to focus. It seems likely that the first time he sees his mother's face and his father's eyes happen when they are asked to identify him at the synagogue. There should be great rejoicing, but there is not. As one pair of eyes is opening, others are closing. The gatekeepers at the synagogue who claim access to God have tunnel vision. They have already decided that this Jesus is not the Christ and that anyone who sees differently will be thrown out, excommunicated. This is the reason the parents are afraid to support their son when interrogated about the nature of his blindness and an explanation for his sight. If, in our need to defend orthodoxy, we close the door to friendship, compassion, and honest inquiry, we will not experience the miracle of new sight for the blind or rejoice when it happens for others. Because they think they already know all the right answers, the Pharisees themselves are blind to new possibilities.[§]

There is a powerful line in the Acts narrative just before Stephen is dragged from the synagogue to be

§ Gustavo: Sadly, this is what religion without relationship does to us. Faithful religious leaders—those who have already defined blindness as a sin—have already defined the means and expressions of God's work in an individual's life. Sometimes we do the same when we develop our exclusionary lists that fit our religious frameworks without considering God's ability to operate in a person in a way that God wants when those whom God wants to touch allow him.

stoned. Luke records that "they were furious and gnashed their teeth at him. They covered their ears and, yelling at the top of their voices, they all rushed at him" (Acts 7:54, 57). When I find myself gnashing my teeth, when I talk more than I listen, when I stop trying to understand, when I refuse to look at what I don't want to see—I need to take a timeout and recognize that I've stopped being an ambassador for Christ. Jesus's final word spoken to the Pharisees in this narrative causes me to "tremble, tremble, tremble," as the old Johnny Cash song says.

With arrogance and contempt they ask, "Are you calling us blind?" (see John 9:40).

Jesus said, "If you were blind, you would not be guilty of sin; but now that you claim you can see, your guilt remains" (v. 41).

It is a beautiful thing to think about the idea that the work of God in our lives starts in God's heart, not ours. The progression to faith in the story of the newly seeing man reflects a pattern that is often the way people come to faith in Christ. The story starts with inclusion and recognition of a need. The man is blind. Compassion leads to redemptive engagement. Jesus is willing to confront the systemic evil of religious practices. In response to being seen and included, the seed of faith is planted and has an opportunity to grow. When asked to choose, the seeing man moves toward love in response to love. When alignment with Jesus becomes more costly, he

§ Gustavo: The final en-
counter of Jesus with the
man born blind sums up
the whole principle that we
are trying to highlight in
this book. The man didn't
belong anywhere. The per-
ceived stigma of his con-
dition as sin alienated him
from society and particularly
from religious life. He didn't
belong anywhere, except
for the heart of Jesus. Jesus
embraced him, despite the
disciples' theological non-
sense and the religious leaders' biases. The man didn't
believe at first, and the best
he could muster when he
was pressured by religious
leaders was to play by their
rules by calling Jesus a
prophet. But when the man
encountered Jesus in his full
dimension, the amazing love
and grace of Jesus made it
irresistible for the man not
to believe. In many of my
encounters with my agnostic
relatives whom I love dearly,
I have decided to stop
arguing faith and theology
with them. I love them and
embrace them, and then

steps toward faith and says, "Nobody has ever heard of opening the eyes of a man born blind. If this man were not from God, he could do nothing" (vv. 32–33). This response gets him thrown out of the synagogue. He identifies with Jesus, but his understanding is not developed. When Jesus hears what happened to him, he seeks and finds him. He asks the question that every evangelism system I ever learned was designed to pose: "Do you believe in the Son of Man?" (v. 35). This is the right question, and it is a necessary ques-tion—it just isn't the leading question. Because of the authentic relationship that is established, the "Lord, I believe" (v. 38) confession that follows is natural and not coerced.§

I met Tanya in Moscow in the summer of 1991 when I traveled to Russia with a group of American youth leaders. Our goal was to purchase one of the Young Pioneer camps that were in the countryside outside the city. Russia's youth camping program, which at its peak boasted 40,000 camps and 9.3 million campers a year, had fallen on hard times by the early 1990s. Rus-sia too had fallen on hard times, and Moscow reflected it. The economy was struggling; opportunities were few. The Cold War that had defined the U.S. relation-ship with Russia had warmed. For the first time in my life travel was open, and so were the people.

We were there to help plant our church and to see if we could purchase one of the Pioneer properties close to the city. We wanted to duplicate the kind of sum-mer ministries that were central to our youth programming in the U.S. There were about twenty of us, and feeding us was a bit of a problem. No restaurants were open—no one could afford to eat in them. Food preparation for a group our size required more than there were volunteers to accomplish it. Our hosts contracted with a nearby restaurant to open twice a day to feed us breakfast and dinner.

Tanya lived close by and, because she had taken English in school, was hired to serve us. Tanya was eighteen, quick-witted, and friendly. We loved her. Americans in general are perceived in other countries as too loud, overconfident, and culturally insensitive. Multiply this by the fact that we were all youth workers, and it should be clear that Tanya had her hands full with us. She was up to the challenge, though, and had all of us eating out of her hand by the time we headed home.

The next summer I was back in Moscow, this time with eighteen high school students and a handful of leaders from Nampa, Idaho, where I was the youth pastor. We were there to develop relationships with youth and children who lived in the area where we were planting a church. This time our hosts hired Tanya to be our translator, tour guide, and babysitter. Because at nineteen she was a bit older than our students and because of life experience, she was street smart. She became like an older sister to our group. It was only a day or two before she was one of us. We counted on her for everything, from how to ride the subway to how to behave at the Kremlin and how

> I pray they will encounter the fullness of Jesus. Such a fullness gives humanity no other option than to believe. The man belonged to the fellowship of Jesus first. Then he believed.

much to pay for those iconic Russian nesting dolls. She belonged, and we loved her absolutely.

When we loaded the buses for the airport to go home, I remember seeing Tanya standing next to Chuck and Carla Sunberg, our church-planting pastors and missionaries who had just arrived in Moscow. I watched as our students said goodbye to Tanya—we would have packed her in our luggage and taken her home with us if we could have. We went home but stayed in touch with Tanya as much as we could.

The following year I ran into Carla at a denominational meeting and asked about Tanya. She'd been offered a job at a nightclub that catered to Americans coming to Moscow to do business. Tonya had made some real steps toward faith, and Carla was concerned that this could be a major setback. When I asked how much she'd be making the figure was large for someone in Moscow but not a lot in U.S. currency. We made a deal on the spot. Carla would hire Tanya to work for the new church plant in Moscow, and our youth group would match the salary she would have made working at the nightclub. Tanya wasn't to know where the money was coming from because it wasn't charity. She belonged to us. And that's what we did. Every Sunday night our youth group prayed for Tanya and collected our love for her in dollars.

During that year she was baptized and made plans to attend our denominational college in Switzerland. She finished her degree and met and married Davide, a student from Sicily. After graduation they moved to Moscow, where, for sixteen years, she pastored the church that was established in the area where our youth group had helped build bridges.

I had the opportunity to video chat with Tanya as I was working on this chapter. Tanya and Davide are opening the work of our church in the city of Minsk, Belarus. I didn't want to overstate the role we had played in her journey to faith and ministry, so I wanted to fact-check my story. As we talked, our memories blended. It was the belonging in those summer days of 1992 that opened doors of faith and established deep bonds of friendship. I am reminded that a sower went out to sow, and some of the seed fell on good soil. This is Tanya's testimony:

> I met the youth from Nampa when I was nineteen. I was nothing like these kids who came as part of the mission team. I'd lived through a lot in nineteen years. Born in the USSR into a typical atheist home, I'd gone through school and then experienced the collapse of the USSR, both economically and politically.
>
> I had to quit the university and get a job at a bar. There used to be a strictly controlled ethos in the Soviet days. That gave way to a new freedom that the youth didn't really know what to do about. It became a do-what-you-like kind of freedom. I worked at the bar of the hotel where the group was staying. I spoke little English but tried. Talking with native English speakers was a lot of fun.

I sought to spend as much time with the Nampa kids as I could. Every day after I was done with my job I would hang out with the team, participating in the summer activities they did for Russian youth. There were games, music in English, Bible stories, and just time to hang out. It was all fascinating. It was so new to me. But, more than anything, I was drawn to these kids because of their absolute openness and acceptance of me. There were no judgments, no moral lessons—just friendship and smiles, and they welcomed me to hang out with them as much as I wanted.

I watched them. I watched how they related to one another, watched them having fun (that involved no alcohol—that was unusual), watched them joking and laughing in clean, non-offensive ways. They were different, and they were loving. I felt accepted by them. I was from a different world, but they made me feel that I belonged. That left a deep imprint on me, and it made me think. Their life and attitude were so different from what I had ever known that it made me ask questions about what they had that I and my Russian friends didn't have.

A year passed after that first encounter before I came to faith in Christ, but the seeds were planted that first summer that I spent with these young Christians. They might have had their own struggles, but they did the best they could, embracing these Soviet kids and making them feel accepted and loved. That became a door wide open to come to know the God who accepts us as we are and then transforms us to be who he created us to be. I would remember that group long after they left, but I didn't know until much later that they didn't forget about me when they left.

When I entrusted my life to Christ and was baptized in 1993, I was faced with new challenges. I quit my job at the hotel bar and was doing summer jobs helping the Nazarene missionaries by taking groups around and helping with activities. But as the summer came to an end, I faced the challenge of finding a new job. It was a struggle trying to practice my faith in Christ and to do what was pleasing to him and finding that the only jobs available seemed to be those that would bring me back to my old lifestyle. I was learning to pray and wanted to be faithful in my Christian walk, but I needed to support myself and my mom. My options were not making me happy.

Then Carla Sunberg asked me to come by, and she offered me work in the church office. The salary was low, but it was comparable to what I had been offered in other places. That was truly an answer to my prayer that allowed me to get rooted deeper in my newfound faith. I was discipled by Chuck and Carla Sunberg and discovered my calling to ministry, which led me to European Nazarene College in 1995.

What I learned years later was that those kids I had met in the summer of 1992 were the ones who provided the money for the Sunbergs to pay my salary, allowing me to stay engaged with the church and not fall back into the life I once lived. I learned this many years after I completed my studies, received an MA from seminary, and had been in ministry for years. All that God had led me through during those years started with a simple act of acceptance by these young Christians, allowing a young Soviet woman to feel like she belonged to them despite being so different, and despite not living up to their standards of faith and morality. Belonging and then believing is definitely the story of my life.

7. BELONGING BEFORE BELIEVING IN HISTORY
The Celtic Way

Stephanie

The cold morning air bit at her fingers and toes as she crept out of bed. The sun was not yet up, but the gray edges of the sky held the promise of light. Ana walked outside to relight the fire, her hands going through the simple, quotidian motion of lifting the peat and stirring the embers. As she worked she prayed:

> *I will kindle my fire this morning*
> *In the presence of the holy angels of heaven*
> *God kindle thou in my heart within*
> *A flame of love to my neighbor*
> *To my foe, to my friend, to my kindred all*
> *To the brave, to the knave, to the thrall . . .*
> *Without malice, without jealousy, without envy*
> *Without fear, without terror of anyone under the*
> *sun.*[16]

---

16. Esther de Waal, *Every Earthly Blessing: Rediscovering the Celtic Tradition* (Harrisburg, PA: Morehouse Publishing, 1999), xvi.

While the task of lighting the fire was not new, the prayer was. She had lived among the Christians for less than a year, working alongside them, learning from them, slowly coming to practice their way of being in the world. What a whirlwind it had all been.

As the smoke rose into the air, she fanned the flickering fire into a steady blaze. The licking flames sent the memories roaring in, and she wondered at how, a year ago, a different fire had been lit. Every other fire in the countryside had been extinguished by order of the Druids in preparation for the festival marking the coming of spring, the balance between light and darkness. The Druids and tribe leaders were gathered to the mansion of King Leoghaire in the Valley of Tara, where an enormous fire would be built. The rest of the commoners—those on the outside of power and position—waited for the smoke to rise that signaled the beginning of the new season. Only then could they relight their own home fires.

Ana had stood, shivering, next to the cold family fire pit, straining her eyes to see any flicker of light in the distant valley. How weary she was of waiting, of being on the outside, of never having access to the secret knowledge of the Druids, of living in fear of danger, superstition, and sacrifice.

Suddenly, a bright light caught her eye—not from the Valley of Tara but from the Hill of Slane. A man stood next to a roaring conflagration, the largest fire she had ever seen. He stood facing the valley in clear defiance of the Druids. With boldness, he marched forward toward the valley, chanting prayers of protection to his God.

Ana's imagination was stirred. Could there be light beyond the darkness of the Druids, who kept their knowledge so hidden from the likes of her? Could there be something beyond the daily struggle to survive, the constant dread of offending a god, the continual fear that perhaps she or her child might be chosen as a sacrifice for the gods?

When the dawn finally broke, Ana took the hand of her husband and child and walked into the Christian monastic community. There were walls surrounding the community, indicating the boundaries, but the gates were wide open, welcoming them in. Life changed immediately. Violence was forbidden within the walls of the community.[17] Food and resources were not hoarded but shared. The daily work was performed in community. Holy men and women openly taught the way of the Christian God to anyone who had interest—there were no secrets.[18] Who was this God who did not demand animal or human sacrifice but rather sacrificed his own Son for her sake and the sake of the world? Who was this God who, unlike the gods of her childhood, did not change like

---

17. George G. Hunter III, *The Celtic Way of Evangelism: How Christianity Can Reach the West . . . Again* (Nashville: Abingdon, 2010), 17.
18. Hunter, *The Celtic Way of Evangelism*, 71.

shifting shadows but offered steadfast, unwavering love and faithfulness?

Her desire to belong to these strange people intensified; her hunger to learn was insatiable. Their way of life was strange yet appealing as she witnessed in them the authentic sign—a congruency between their words of hope and their lives.

Today, a year later, she would be baptized in the name of the Father, Son, and Holy Spirit—the triune God she had come to trust with her life. Nothing would ever be the same, and how grateful she was for that. She, the welcomed, would now become the welcoming as she invited others to experience the life she had found.

Patrick and His Mission

While Ana's story is fictional, it is based on historical events, including St. Patrick's confrontation with pagan Druids of Ireland and the dramatic evangelistic movement of the Celtic Church. In the late fourth century, Patrick was a nominally Christian English teenager, happily living a life of ease. His life changed dramatically when he was kidnapped and sold as a slave in Ireland, where he worked for his master, Milchu, for seven years.[19] During that time, he came

---

19. James H. Todd, *St. Patrick, Apostle of Ireland: A Memoir of His Life and Mission* (Eugene, OR: Wipf & Stock Publishers, 2003), 374.

to know the Lord in a new way and described his daily work in the fields as precious times of communion and prayer. Not only did Patrick come to know the Lord in a profound way, but he also came to know the Irish, their culture, and their language.

Patrick eventually escaped through the guidance of the Holy Spirit and returned home. Years later, God spoke to Patrick through a dream. The Irish called out to Patrick in the dream, asking, "We pray thee, holy youth, to come and henceforth walk among us."[20] Patrick responded to the call of God and returned to the land of his captivity to share the gospel with the people who would become his very own.§

At this time, the church was still united under the leadership of Rome because neither the schism between East and West nor the Protestant Reformation had occurred. The Roman Empire, though in decline, was far-reaching. In every place it had conquered, it imported its culture, values, and way of life. The church adopted this model, insisting that converts leave behind their "barbarian" ways and life to adopt the Roman way of life. To be Christian was to be Roman.[21]

Ireland, though it traded with Rome, was not under Roman rule and therefore maintained its distinct

§ Gustavo: My experience as a missionary has been that our call is a combination of our personal experience of Christ in us and a deep sense of the impact that community and culture have on us and on society. Just like Patrick, the depth and efficacy of our ministry depend not only on the depth of our pious life (our love of God with all our heart, soul, mind, and strength) but also on the love and understanding that we have for our fellow humans.

---

20. Todd, *St. Patrick*, 377.
21. Hunter, *The Celtic Way of Evangelism*, 7.

culture.[22] Patrick, intimately familiar with this culture, rejected the idea that becoming a Christian meant becoming Roman. He sought not to convert Irish culture to Roman culture but to redeem Irish culture under the lordship of Jesus. Patrick did not, for example, condemn the Celtic adoration of nature but sought to steer their attention to the Creator of the world they adored. He honored the Celtic view of interconnectedness of all things but helped them see God as the heart—the Sustainer and Redeemer. The Celtic cross, a circle imposed upon a traditional Roman cross, represents this redeemed worldview. The circle, representing the "great O of creation,"[23] is bound to the cross of redemption. God's good creation and God's redemptive purpose are inextricably intertwined.

In *The Celtic Way of Evangelism,* George Hunter III outlines the contrast between the Roman way of evangelism and the Celtic model practiced by Patrick and his successors: "Bluntly stated, the Roman model for reaching people . . . is this: (1) present the Christian message; (2) invite them to decide to believe in Christ and become Christians; and (3) if they decide positively, welcome them into the church and its fellowship." He contrasts this with the Celtic model: "(1) establish community with people or bring them into the fellowship of your community of faith; (2) within

---

22. De Waal, *Every Earthly Blessing,* 20.
23. De Waal, *Every Earthly Blessing,* xiii.

fellowship, engage in conversation, ministry, prayer, and worship; and (3) in time, as they discover they now believe, invite them to commit."[24]

The Roman model targeted the mind almost exclusively. It assumed that the logic and methods of Roman culture translated with no remainder to a passionate, earthy Celtic soul. Patrick knew otherwise. His concern was not with control and conformity to the Roman way. He rejected the idea that the Christian faith was only accessible to the literate, culturally Roman person, instead embracing the truth that God loved the "barbarian" Celts as they were. Patrick's mission was clear—to share the transformative gospel of Christ—but he held the methods loosely so that he might be able to communicate the gospel to this unique culture he deeply loved in a way that it might be heard.

Wherever he went, Patrick began his work not with an appeal to logic to the unconverted masses but rather by establishing a community of believers in the midst of the pagan Celts. These communities practiced Christian living together through sharing, learning, and peaceful living. Philip Sheldrake describes the intention of these communities as serving as the "anticipation of paradise" in which the good intentions of God for creation might be experienced

---

24. Hunter, *The Celtic Way of Evangelism*, 42.

and practiced by women and men.[25] The communities modeled an alternative way of being in a culture marked by violence and division. They declared by their communal practice of generosity, love, and inclusion, *This is God's desire for creation—restoration, healing, and love! You are welcome here.* Hunter notes that the walls surrounding these communities "did not signify an enclosure to keep out the world" but rather indicated the space in which this alternative life would be practiced.[26]

Its Gates Will Never Be Shut

In Revelation 21, we are given a vision of the city of God. It needs no temple because God dwells among the people. Nor does it need sun or moon, for the glory of the Lord is its light. And best of all, "its gates will never be shut" (v. 25, NRSV) as people come bringing "the glory and the honor of the nations" (v. 26, NRSV). The intention of God is the inclusion of all who would come and live in the kingdom way. So too with Patrick's community. *Come and belong! Taste and see that the Christian God is good. Come and live the kingdom way with us.* Patrick and his fellow believers created kingdom communities of belonging.

These communities of belonging were marked by several distinct characteristics. First, as has already

---

25. Philip Sheldrake, *Living Between Worlds: Place and Journey in Celtic Spirituality* (Boston: Cowley Publications, 1995), 38–39.
26. Hunter, *The Celtic Way of Evangelism*, 17.

been mentioned, the communities practiced an alternative way of being in the world. The Celts were known as vicious warriors in battle, even decapitating their enemies. To exist as a nonviolent community in imitation of their crucified and risen Lord, the Celtic Christians declared, *This is kingdom territory.* Those who had lived under the dark cloud of violence and retribution found a place of peace and rest.

The hagiography of the saints often includes stories of saints being cared for by wild animals during periods of seclusion. One story even tells of a wolf who cared for and nurtured a cow.[27] Although these tales are apocryphal in nature, they speak to a larger truth: redemption is not only saving souls for heaven; it is the restoration of heaven on earth. It is a vision of creation healed and renewed. According to Hunter, "For the Celtic apostles, Jesus Christ comes to restore our humanity and to complete his good creation."[28]

In addition to modeling an alternative way of life, Celtic Christian communities were indigenous in nature. Kingdom communities took on a distinct Celtic color that was reflected in the very fabric of the community. As Celts perceived the spiritual in the commonplace and were attuned to the created order, Patrick and others in the Christian communities wrote prayers for every aspect of life, from starting

27. De Waal, *Every Earthly Blessing*, 77.
28. Hunter, *The Celtic Way of Evangelism*, 85.

the morning fire to milking the cow. Every aspect of life bore the blessing of God's presence, down to the most mundane chore. Common items and experiences communicated the grace of God. Patrick is famously known for using a shamrock to explain the Trinity. Though his illustration was later determined to be a demonstration of the heresy of partialism, the intent remains: using what is near and familiar to explain the weighty things of God so that others might come to know God.

Finally, the Celtic Christians created communities of belonging by exercising their imaginations and encouraging those who sought belonging to do the same. Imagine if we lived into God's vision for us. Imagine if we rejected violence, revenge, and destruction. Imagine if we gave ourselves fully to caring for one another and for creation. What could be? Hunter once again says it well: "[The Celtic Christians] seem to have believed that if you could make a Christian truth claim clear to the people's imaginations, the people and the Holy Spirit would take it from there, especially if they were already tasting Christian community."[29]

Now What?

Having tasted Christian community and experienced authentic belonging, the time comes to ask the

---

29. Hunter, *The Celtic Way of Evangelism*, 67.

question, "Does their story hold fast? Is this Jesus who they say he is?" The Celtic Christians did not so much *make* truth claims as they *embodied* truth claims. They knew Jesus to be Lord and thus surrendered their lives to him entirely.

Drawing from Aristotle and Kenneth Burke, Hunter recognizes two factors that made Celtic Christians and their message trustworthy: ethos and identification. First, the ethos of the Celtic Christians was one of integrity. What they said matched what they did. Their beliefs shaped how they lived together, from the most ordinary to the holiest of tasks. There was no false dichotomy between secular and sacred. All life belonged to God, a truth reflected in every aspect of their shared life.

It would be easy to romanticize Celtic Christian communities and imagine they had none of the inner turmoil and challenges of contemporary churches, which was clearly not the case. However, they were recognized as people in whom there was no guile or deceit. There was no sense that Celtic Christians pursued power over or control of others. This humility and congruence of life made their message trustworthy.

Second, the Celtic Christians identified with their pagan sisters and brothers. There was no "us versus them." There was only "we"—wounded sinners in need of healing and forgiveness. Celtic Christians identified with those not yet part of the faith, acknowledging and expressing empathy for their struggles, fears, and desires. Their identification was strengthened by their practice of incarnation, entering into the experience of others for their good. This was not a ministry strategy so much as it was the pursuit of the faithful expression of incarnational love modeled by God's self in Christ.

The message of the Celtic Christians was believable because of their ethos of congruence and their identification with those with whom they sought to share their faith. Hunter, expounding on ideas from both Aristotle and Ralph Waldo Emerson, referred to this as an "authentic sign"—believability based on intelligence, character, and goodwill.[30] The Celtic Christians knew the story of God, their lives reflected its truth, and they were *for* their listeners, desiring them to experience the transformative love of God. This authentic sign, in partnership with the experience of authentic belonging, stirred imaginations all the more, inspiring belief.

With their imaginations stirred through genuine belonging and the authentic sign of the Celtic Christians, many pagans came to know and trust Jesus with their lives. Having given themselves to belief, the *behavior* of these new followers of Jesus was changed. Prior to their conversion, Celts understood the spiritual world to be intertwined with the physical world. Nothing was beyond the realm of the

30. Hunter, *The Celtic Way of Evangelism*, 49.

divine. They marked what were understood as "thin spaces"—physical spaces with standing stones called *menhirs*. "Whenever a menhir rises it indicates an earthly centre where the lower, earth, and man, can link with higher, with the cosmos and the gods."[31] Newly converted Celtic Christians did not abandon this integrated worldview. Rather, their worldview was converted as well. Instead of raising *menhirs*, Celtic Christians now raised enormous crosses across the countryside—the great Celtic cross indicating the intersection of creation and redemption.

Other aspects of the lives of new converts took on new meaning. As Esther de Waal writes, mundane tasks such as churning the butter or driving the herds were done with great care and excellence. "Work is, after all, a matter of partnership with him, something through which [God] may be better known."[32] Relationships were transformed as well. Intertribal wars ceased. Slavery was eventually outlawed under Patrick's leadership.[33] Human sacrifices ended as people came to know the God who sacrificed his Son for the sake of the world. Ultimately, following Jesus resulted in a transferal of allegiance. No longer were people

---

31. Jerry C. Doherty, *A Celtic Model of Ministry: The Reawakening of Community Spirituality* (Collegeville, MN: Liturgical Press, 2003), 42.

32. De Waal, *Every Earthly Blessing*, 15.

33. Thomas Cahill, *How the Irish Saved Civilization: The Untold Story of Ireland's Heroic Role from the Fall of Rome to the Rise of Medieval Europe* (New York: Anchor Books, 1996), 110.

bound to their tribes and the violence associated with those loyalties. They surrendered that allegiance in order to give themselves in devotion to following their new Lord, Jesus Christ.

Having undergone transformation in every aspect of their lives, new Celtic Christians became part of the mission. They did not simply remain in their communities, soaking in goodness and blessing. They ventured out into the Irish countryside, traveling in bands of believers and making their home with other tribes. They modeled the belonging they had received, demonstrating the "authentic sign" through their ethos of congruency and sincere identification with the people. They taught with authority and power and demonstrated what a life transformed by Christ could be. Over only a few generations, the majority of Ireland had come to know Christ without bloodshed.

The Contemporary Church

Though our context is different from the fifth-century Celts, there are notable parallels. The "pagan" population—those who hold no religious views or those with views beyond the mainline religions—has increased. Biblical literacy, along with previous cultural markers associated with the Bible and Christianity, is low—even nonexistent—among many. Mass media, conspiracy theories, and easy access to significant platforms by anyone with an idea regardless of veracity or reliability have left people cynical and skeptical. We are a people in need of an authentic sign.

What do Patrick and the Celtic Church have to teach us in the twenty-first century? We, the authors, are not innovators out to create yet another strategy that will save the church—this time for good. We are observers of history, paying particular attention to eras in which God did something remarkable among God's people. The era of Patrick and the Celts, and the subsequent generations, is one such notable period. What can we learn from our ancient sisters and brothers?

Belonging

Like the Celts, we are called to create communities of belonging. Like the ancient monasteries of Ireland, we have walls that set our communities apart as unique spaces in which we anticipate the kingdom of God. However, our gates shall never be shut. There is no entry fee to be part of the Christian community. Whoever wishes to explore the community and experience the life of faith may come and be welcomed without reserve. This presumes, of course, that the community of faith is in fact living as an anticipation of the kingdom of God as empowered by the Holy Spirit. The Christian community must model an alternative way of being that is practiced beyond the church. Partisanship, division, violence, greed, pride, and selfishness have no place among the people of God. Those behaviors are reflective of a culture in need of redemption and healing; they are not the "natural" result of being human. Our humanity is redeemed and sanctified as we respond to the Spirit's movement among us. The community must strive toward becoming a safe haven from the vitriol and violence of society in order that, by the power of the Spirit, our communities might become a foretaste of the kingdom of God as we love and serve. The result is a spacious place where those who seek might find hope and healing.

An invitation into this spacious place stirs the imagination. It inspires the question, *What might my life become? Could it be hope-filled, joyful, brimming with purpose?* Imagination is central to creating communities of belonging and building a bridge to belief. No proposition can inspire hope like a vision of a life transformed. A proposition does not free us from violence and fear. A proposition does not heal us from wounds or guilt from the past. But a clear vision of what life could be? A glimpse into a different way of being? The imagination inspires and breathes hope into what feels irredeemable.

In addition to attending to the imagination, kingdom communities of belonging must be indigenous. Creating communities that are reflective of the existing culture is not the same thing as acquiescing to the values of the surrounding society. It is the acknowledgment that God is present in every culture, speaking and revealing God's self. It is also the recognition that every culture is in need of redemption. No culture is inherently Christian. All must be redeemed. This realization frees us from the need to reshape a culture in our image. Like Patrick, we seek to name the holy around us. What thin places might be acknowledged as holy ground? What standing stones might become crosses? It is not a purging of culture but a healing, a redemption.

Finally, communities of belonging are incarnational. This has become a buzzword in many circles and has, unfortunately, lost its punch. To be incarnational is not merely to spend time with the people we hope to introduce to Jesus, though that is important. Nor is it simply familiarizing oneself with local traditions, values, or customs. It is a complete immersion in people and culture. It is the taking on of the flesh of the people among whom we live. Patrick left England behind and did not turn back. It might be said that he surrendered his nationality and many of the privileges therein and became Irish for the sake of the gospel. His deep love for the people moved him to live among them as they lived for the rest of his life. Ultimately, we look to Christ as the model of faithful incarnation. As Gregory Nazianzen said, "What has not been assumed has not been healed." Thus, our Lord assumed human flesh and nature to heal us and deliver us to God. How can we not do the same for the sake of those we have been called to love and serve?

Authentic belonging in a kingdom community sets the stage for belief, but in the end, the community of faith trusts the Spirit to transform and redeem. There is no fear-driven evangelism but, rather, a hope-filled posture of patience and love. There is an invitation that says, *Come and live among us, in this kingdom community. Come to know this triune God who has made a way for our salvation.*

Believing, Behaving, Becoming

Having welcomed others to belong to our kingdom community of faith, we now invite them to believe. It is essential that we remember that belonging cannot be contingent upon a person coming to belief. If a person is rejected by the community because they do not come to faith—whether according to our timeline or at all—we have reduced the radical inclusion of God to a meager method, a manipulative strategy of evangelism. Belief cannot come to bear on belonging. However, we also do people a disservice if we do not invite them to step beyond belonging into transformative belief.

The message of the Celts was believable because the people modeled the *authentic sign*—that true and steadfast congruence of proclamation and life. The primary lesson we give to those who would believe is the way in which we practice our faith in every aspect of our lives. Is there congruence between what we say, who we are, and what we do? This congruence further awakens the imagination already inspired by the witness of the kingdom community of belonging.

As we live toward being an authentic sign, modeling the transformative power of belief, we proclaim this triune God—the agent of transformation, healing, and forgiveness. This proclamation must be accessible and contextual. Though we shake our heads at the legend surrounding Patrick's ultimately heretical teaching around the shamrock, we must take pause and recognize his purpose, which was to communicate the gospel in a way that was accessible to his listeners. How might our surrounding context proclaim the gospel, if we have eyes to see? How might we use language that makes sense to our listeners, even as we teach them the holy language of faith? This is not a pandering to relevance; it is the holy work of finding ourselves in the story of God so that our own story might be transformed.

Ultimately, belief is a surrender to the lordship of Christ in every facet of our lives. It is less a mental assent to a series of propositions and more a transferal of allegiance. Our allegiance shifts from self and our sin-sick nature to the person of Jesus, who leads us toward healing and forgiveness, that we might be whole.

Having found belonging among the people of God and, having surrendered to the lordship of Jesus, our lives are changed. We cannot live as before, nor do we want to. We no longer desire simply to belong to the community of faith or even merely believe in Jesus; we long for our lives to reflect our new name: *Christian.* For the Celts, that meant a rejection of

> § Gustavo: The Celtic Way is a reminder that God has always been in the business of restoring his creation by renewing his church—the vehicle that he instituted to share the good news of salvation and redemption in Jesus Christ. Throughout the history of the church, every time that the church becomes over-institutionalized, focusing on methodology and human standards of salvation and belonging, God's Holy Spirit redirects God's church. Patrick was used as God's instrument to show the church that nominal religion, while institutionally and financially powerful, cannot transform the depths of darkness and paganism of societies. By reinstating the incarnational, all-embracing model of Jesus's ministry, an entire nation was saved. I pray that the Lord help us reorient the church so we can reinstate the loving model of Jesus in our midst so that the church can continue being Christ to others.

violence, tribal warfare, and the secret knowledge and sacrifices associated with Druidism. We must attune our communal ears to the Spirit as we seek to discern what practices and loyalties we must surrender to the lordship of Jesus. As an act of loving devotion, we walk in newness of life alongside our Christian community.

The final step in the progression of discipleship is the decision to become—to enter into covenant with a specific community of believers. To become a member of a specific tradition is to assert, *I believe in the unique mission of this body of believers and choose to participate in that mission.* Such a commitment demands a surrender of individualism in that it asks us to enter into covenants of character and conduct for the sake of the community at large. It is not an exercise in legalism but a declaration that the good of the whole supersedes the desires and preferences of the individual. Our becoming is both decision and grace, a response to God's call into a particular community.

Conclusion

We give thanks for the faithful who have gone before us.§ We learn from their sacrificial obedience and loving devotion. However, we seek not to duplicate their work. Rather, we allow their witness to ignite our imaginations for what might be in our own contexts. As we discern how we might grow into kingdom communities of belonging that inspire others toward

believing, behaving, and becoming, may we pray
alongside our ancient brother Patrick:

> *May the strength of God pilot us,*
> *May the wisdom of God instruct us,*
> *May the hand of God protect us,*
> *May the word of God direct us.*
> *May thy salvation, O Lord, be always ours this*
> *day and for evermore.*[34]

---

34. The Leo House, "An Old Irish Blessing for St. Patrick's Day," https://leohousenyc.com/2017/03/15/st-patricks-day-prayer-irish-blessing/.

8. WHAT DOES THIS MEAN FOR THE CHURCH TODAY?

We have journeyed together through the reflection of three different writers, ministers, and thinkers. As different as all three of us are, we faithfully believe that our unifying thoughts can help reorient the church to continue being the welcoming, loving, embracing, discipling, and maturing church that Christ intended. Using the same interactive format as previous chapters, we asked Stephanie to lead us in this final chapter in a virtual roundtable so we can together bring our thoughts to a practical conclusion for the local church today. The following interaction is the summary of our conclusions as they apply to the local church.

∫ Stephanie

What does it look like to create a culture of belonging in ministry context?

† Jerry

Churches with an inward focus will not fulfill the Great Commission and will consequently have no sustainable future. The first step is a mindset—a decision that we're not just going to be looking after our own interests but that we are going to be interested in the needs of others. This mindset decision doesn't have to be either/or. Dallas Willard warns of the danger of a church being overly outwardly focused and ignoring discipleship, and that is a legitimate concern. But if we are truly the disciples of Jesus, then we will be concerned about the same things he is concerned about and will follow his pattern for ministry. While he spent much of his time with the development of the twelve, it wasn't just for their benefit—there was always a gospel focus. So a belonging culture is a matter of the heart, a decision to include. This should be a focus of our collective prayer.

People looking at us from the outside expect us to be unselfish like Jesus. This is one reason the church has received so much criticism and scorn lately—a self-centered church is an untenable contradiction. In the United States churches are granted nonprofit, tax-exempt status, and they don't pay property tax because they have always been considered to be an asset to the community. But if the church only sees itself as existing for the benefit and protection of its own, then we should give up our claim to exemption because we were given that designation on the basis that we were good for the community.

Current circumstances give us so many opportunities. There are so many needs, and with just a little imagination and intention, we can be of service to our neighbors and communities, reflecting the love of Christ. We have a chance to change the narrative.

∫ Stephanie

I do believe it's a bit of a false dichotomy to say we have to pit discipleship against outreach, and I think you would agree with that, Jerry. I don't think it's either/or but both/and as healthy churches are continually doing both.

When I think about creating a culture of belonging, I'm first drawn to leadership. What does it look like to cultivate that spirit of belonging in our leadership—whether church staff or the board/council, or other lay leaders? I think back to experiences I've had in ministry. There were times when I took risks in terms of allowing people to participate and contribute to ministry even when they were still organically moving toward Christ but hadn't necessarily had a conversion moment yet. I chose to take a risk and allowed a person to serve and engage with the hope and prayer that they would be formed by the community in a way that would lead them to a transformational experience with Christ. And, often, they were.

With our leadership, we can demonstrate that culture of belonging as we ourselves model it in how we spend our time, energy, and resources in a way that reflects that value. It's one thing to say we value belonging. It's another thing to look at how we steward our time and resources. If they are exclusively internal or even exclusively external, we're not cultivating that environment where discipleship can take place. I think that speaks to our priorities more than anything we say.

§ Gustavo

To me, a belonging church is a discipling church. A belonging church is a church that understands that discipleship begins even before people know they are part of a journey of grace. It starts when we see people as disciples regardless of their confession of faith or conviction. We allow God's prevenient grace to work in people as they are discipled. A belonging church is also a church that understands that evangelism is part of the discipleship journey. In fact, discipleship without a component of evangelism is not real discipleship in the same way that discipleship without an element of welcoming is not real discipleship. But to reach that point of being a welcoming church, there are some areas of recognition we need to work into the church at all levels.

First, we need to recognize that the mission of the church is to be the agent of reconciliation. This is what the apostle Paul taught the Corinthians when he suggested that God is appealing to others through us with the message of reconciliation (see 2 Corinthians 5:19–20). So the first thing is for the church to recognize that we are the instruments of the mission of God to the people, and in that capacity we see the world from a different perspective. We do not judge or preselect to predetermine those who are welcome to our fellowship.

Second, each church must develop among its members a clear recognition of the work of grace in the lives of the believers. If all of us recognize that we are part of the body of Christ because of God's grace and not because of our merits or because we deserve it, then we will see the world differently, without judgment and with a welcoming spirit. This is what the apostle Paul reminds the Corinthians again when he tells them that we are so compelled by the love of Christ because we are convinced that he died so that we all could live—not because we deserved it but because he loved us (see 2 Corinthians 5:14–15). So, if we do not understand the value of grace, we don't preach grace in our churches. If we only preach feel-good Christianity, or if we only preach holier-than-thou Christianity, then we're going to lose touch of the fact that all of us were dead but, because of God's grace, we're alive. When we recognize the mission of the church and the value of grace in our lives, we no longer see people with the carnal, ethnocentric, self-righteous eyes of society. We look at the world differently, through the eyes of Jesus. We see everyone as potential beneficiaries of God's grace.

Third, we need to recognize that there's going to be tension between welcoming the person and welcoming their behaviors, whatever those behaviors are. In that tension we need to recognize that Christ loved every sinner—but he did not celebrate their every behavior that resulted in their being distanced from God's design for their lives.

∫ Stephanie

I think the challenge, or the frustration, that I and others have experienced is that there seems to be a toleration of certain sinful behaviors—particularly when those who exhibit them have been part of the church for a long time—and a more clear rejection of sins we might see in those who are still outside the church. That inconsistency is off-putting to those on the outside who might see unaddressed dissension and discord within the church. Some might see systemic issues in the church, such as the refusal to acknowledge and address systemic racism, or the fact that many congregations are beholden to a political platform in an idolatrous way. The failure of the church to address its own sin and complicity in sinful structures makes the tension we claim to experience between belonging and behavior ring hollow.

† Jerry

What we are trying to describe in this book is a pattern of discipleship that is relationship- and action-oriented. Too often we have made the discipleship process information-driven, as if an inductive Bible study or a notebook and seminar are how disciples are made. Jesus was much more of a trail guide than he was an academician. The disciples learned by following Jesus and doing what he did. This is the discipleship process we are looking for, but it requires that the most mature believers in the congregation take the lead and guide the way.

I love Stephanie's chapter on Celtic Christianity. It made me hungry to know more because that seems to be the right model: *Come and join us and live with us and see how we live.* This kind of discipleship only works, though, if we actually live differently from the world around us. It calls for those people who are the leaders of the church to take seriously their role as followers of Jesus.

I had a good friend in my early days of ministry tell me that the best way to lead and encourage discipleship was to "hold the crown over their heads until they grow into it." I know that kind of positive encouragement is the way I like to be led. It is compelling and motivating when we hear someone we respect talking about the person they believe we are and who we have the capacity to become.

∫ Stephanie

There are interesting implications to saying, *Come and live among us. Come and experience life alongside us. Let's do this together.* There are programmatic implications because if we say, *Just come and sit through a service with us once a week,* that is not an invitation to live alongside. There need to be programmatic changes in how we spend our time and resources that reflect an invitation to come and live alongside, whether that is through shared meals or shared experiences, affinity groups, etc. There are a lot of programmatic implications that indicate our commitment to come and live alongside us.

§ Gustavo

The Celtic experience is a good example of a welcoming church and its missiological implications. But if you want an example of something that works in every culture and for every generation, the first-century church is a good model. If we look at the church as described in the second and fourth chapters of Acts, we see that this church grew because of their behavior and their testimony. The welcoming behavior of the church created the atmosphere in which "the Lord added to their number daily those who were being saved" (2:47).

From the model of the first-century church, we see that the first-century Christians exhibited true Communion (see v. 42), true compassion (see vv. 44–45), true worship (see vv. 46–47), and true community witness (see v. 47). It was natural and organic, and as a result, people felt welcomed. The believers "enjoyed the favor of all the people" (v. 47). So it is no wonder that thousands of them wanted to join the movement of God among them!

This is the true meaning of attraction evangelism. It is not that the church develops schemes to attract people to come and see our well-designed programs and performances. It is not that the church develops methods to compete with the entertainment industry so that people feel attracted to our building. On the contrary, the lesson from the first-century church is that the organically welcoming environment the Holy Spirit enabled them to foster was the result of a contagious lifestyle. They started "adding to their number daily" because their collective lifestyle made the church attractive. Furthermore, their lifestyle did not compromise the core of the message that Jesus is Lord. Their lifestyle did not deviate from Christ's mission for the church to reach the last, the least, and the lost.

† Jerry

One way to accomplish this is to create opportunities for people to join us in service to others. One example that came to mind is a mission trip where we invited a dentist who wasn't a believer to come along. We were going to be doing medical work, and he was a friend of a doctor who was joining us. The normal way of putting together a trip like that is to have an application that ensures everyone is a believer and is prepared to share a testimony of faith. But we often miss faith-building opportunities by not allowing people to participate and offer a gift of service before they come to faith. This dentist only came to participate because of a desire to help people in need, but he ended up actively participating in Bible study and worship as well. So one good way to begin is to create places where people can join us without preconditions.

∫ Stephanie

That's a helpful transition to our second question: how do we create meaningful opportunities for belief and behavior, even as we cultivate this culture of belonging? We don't want to stall out in the belonging. We want to continue to press forward toward belief and transformation of heart and life. So what does it look like to create opportunities for that transition?

§ Gustavo

We have affirmed that one model is to create platforms, or environments, for people to come and feel welcome among us. Another model is Christ's original design for the church—for us to go out and reach out to people in their context and their environment.

The model of the apostle Paul as he visited the Areopagus in Athens is a good example of that approach (see Acts 17:16–34). In reality, Paul did not expect the Epicureans and the Stoics—the equivalents to the postmodern thinkers of our times—to visit him in his synagogue. One of the paradoxes we have in our missiology today is to assume that to be effective we need to make only our church a welcoming place. We have gone so far as to state that the problem of contemporary Christianity is that people don't go to church anymore. But that's not true. The real problem is that the church is not going to the people anymore.

The church was always meant to be a *going* church. A welcoming church has always been an incarnational church that goes to and moves into the neighborhood. When we move into the neighborhood and engage with the people, we help the church become an agent of transformation. We realize that the gospel becomes alive in the lives of those with whom we interact, and this has a transformational effect on the lives of our congregations. When we go to transform the world for Christ, we end up being transformed like Christ.

∫ Stephanie

This demands of us a humility of mind and spirit to enter into genuine dialogue. Too often, we come to those conversations with the mindset, *I have this message, and I'm going to give it to you. I need not listen to you because I have the sole truth.* We often say we want a dialogue, but what we really want is to deliver a monologue. To enter transformative dialogue with someone outside the church requires that we go with a posture of humility, graciousness, and a commitment to listening and learning even when it's uncomfortable.

§ Gustavo

That was exactly what Patrick did in Ireland. He went to his people. He went out, and he was with them with a learning posture. Through that listening and learning posture he was able to share the unspoiled message of Christ with his people and accomplish God's mission.

♪ Stephanie

Well, he deviated from some of the traditions of the church that had sent him. He found ways to say, "This is actually a cultural construct and not a gospel construct." He was able to move past some of those cultural constructs to say, "What does it look like to follow Jesus, in this moment, in this space, in this culture?" He focused on the message and the mission but was willing to let go of many methods and cultural constructs he had inherited.

† Jerry

One of the things that requires some reevaluation is the way we view ministry. As a pastor I was always trying to help people find their ministry opportunity at the church. It takes a lot of volunteer time to facilitate the programs of an active church. Most of my generation has defined ministry as what you do *at* the church. So when we ask someone, "What's your ministry?" we mean, what do you do to make church work? Do you teach Sunday school? Are you an usher or on the music team? If we turn that around, which is what we *must* do if the church is to have a gospel influence in our communities, we will need a broader definition of ministry. We will always need people to make the activities of church work, but we must not devalue the sacred nature of the work people do away from the programs of the church.

When I was entering ministry, there was a lot of talk about full-time Christian service. It is healthy that we don't make that distinction much anymore. We are all full-time Christians, no matter what we do vocationally. For most of the years I served as a pastor, my wife was a high school teacher. Though she always had a place of service at the church, I was grateful that the congregation understood that her primary ministry was to her students and the faculty where she taught. It was common to see people from her school show up at church on Sunday morning because of her influence during the week. To get where we need to go, we need to honor and encourage the ministry of people where they live and work.

∫ Stephanie

There was a man at our former church who served on our board. He chose to step down so he could serve on the local school board instead. Although I was sad to lose his presence on the church board, I was proud of his choice to invest in the community in a meaningful way, and of course he continued to serve the church in other ways. Being on a school board is not a glamorous job. You get a lot of difficult feedback and have to have uncomfortable conversations. Yet he was willing to serve. He was going into the community beyond the walls of the church building and seeking the welfare of our city in a tangible way. It was a wonderful way for him to go out into the world in the name of Jesus and effect positive change.

† Jerry

That reminds me of a book I read—*Lessons from the East: Finding the Future of Western Christianity in the Global Church*, by Bob Roberts, Jr.—that challenged the way we operate our churches in Western culture. He made the case that in the West we pour most of our energy into making Sunday activities the focus of our attention. In other cultures around the world, where the gospel is effectively reaching people, the focus is reversed. The gathering on Sunday is focused on preparing people to be disciples in the places where they have influence throughout the week. I think sometimes in the U.S. we've had it backwards. We focus our attention on getting together for an hour or two a week and haven't always taken church to the community.

∫ Stephanie

Two things come to mind for me, the first being—and I've already alluded to this—modeling; living in such a way that reflects Christ. That demands that our lives be open instead of maintaining a facade that suggests that my life is okay and everything is simple. That is false. Modeling requires actually allowing people into your life in a meaningful way and allowing them into the discord, the frustration, and even the pain and grief of life. What does it look like to be a Christian in the weeds of life? What does it look like to be faithful to God when I lose my job? What does it look like to be faithful to God when my kid gets sick? What does it look like to be faithful to God when I'm facing a conflict? Those questions cannot be answered with words. The answer must be witnessed through modeling and our faithful practice, which demands we allow others into our lives. It demands humility and vulnerability, two things we don't often model well in the church.

Second, it also hinges on faithful teaching and preaching—proclaiming the gospel and teaching Scripture in concert with the tradition of the church. As we preach and teach, we allow the Spirit to do that transformative work. Setting a timeline on a person's transformation or simply delivering a to-do list for being a Christian is the wrong approach. I'm less concerned about the effectiveness of this approach in changing behavior and more concerned that such an approach does not truly produce the transformational heart change we're talking about. We cannot shortcut the transformational process through legalism. No culturally shaped to-do list can transform a heart. Only the Spirit can do that. So faithful teaching and preaching that creates room for the Spirit to work, along with humble, vulnerable modeling, cultivate the space in which the Spirit can truly do some of that transformational work over time.

§ Gustavo

This has a clear implication for how we disciple others. Yes, we need to go back to the discipleship question. Perhaps one of the best ways to help believers grow to become like Christ is to bring back to our churches the role of the mentor. We need to rediscover the value of mentorship in the lives of all believers. Paul's instructions to Timothy were not just to develop new leaders in the church. In his letter to Timothy, Paul encouraged him to pass on the life lessons he had learned from Paul to interested people so they would pass it on to others, and so on (2 Timothy 2:2). Our contemporary discipleship models have relied basically on cognitive development of the Word of God. This Western model of instruction is heavily influenced by the Sophistic method that generates a lot of thought and opinion but very little life modeling. In reality, the first-century church relied as much on mentoring as it did on cognitive development of Scripture.

When Paul said, "imitate me as I imitate Christ" (see 1 Corinthians 11:1), he was highlighting the importance of mentoring in the spiritual and behavioral development of believers. This idea will have implications for the way we go about discipleship of new believers. It means we need to find, equip, and develop mature, vulnerable, sensitive, and experienced believers who are willing to journey with new believers in open, vulnerable, steady modeling until they in turn become disciplers themselves. They become the ones who will train other new believers. This model will help believers collectively and individually move from belonging to believing and from believing to behaving so that entire congregations become, in unity, like Christ.

† Jerry

The churches that are most successful at reaching millennials are the ones that have a practical application of Christianity. It is encouraging that younger people want to actually *see* the church doing something that is making a difference in the lives of others. A good example is one of our churches that has a Buddy Break program designed for people who have children with special needs. Sometimes these parents are giving round-the-clock care to their children and never get a break. Buddy Break is designed for those parents to have a "buddy" for their child so they can have a day to go shopping or fully participate in a worship service. This kind of compassionate approach to ministry is effective in both meeting the need and developing the church.

∫ Stephanie

In addition, consider Generation Z. They want to effect positive change in culture, and they believe they can. They are deeply engaged with social issues on various platforms, whether social media or otherwise. In some ways, Gen Z can really highlight some of the church's blind spots to broken systems and injustice. As Gustavo said, we can focus so myopically on the cognitive and fail to recognize some of the social constructs that are destructive and, frankly, are of empire. The passion of new generations can call us to be the church in faithful ways by naming inconsistencies and the ways in which we participate in systemic inequity and disorder.

This is not unique to Gen Z. It happens in every generation. Each generation must learn in humility from the wisdom of those who have come before, but the church can also draw from and learn from the energy and passion of our young people who come up and say, "I see this and want to effect change." The church can either reject their idealism as the ignorance of youth, or the church can say, "Let's be part of that in a faithful, Christ-shaped way. Let's learn and walk together to practice the way of the kingdom in this time and place." The generations can edify and strengthen one another to bring wholeness and healing to the church.

§ Gustavo

That was the behavior of the first-century church. As a result of their lifestyle and testimony, they enjoyed favor with the people.

∫ Stephanie

Here is our final question. We've alluded to this a bit already, but what does it look like for pastors to express leadership in a church and bring the church along in this transition away from "you must believe and behave and become, and then you can belong"? What does it look like for pastors to lead their churches into this paradigm shift?

§ Gustavo

In practical terms, I see at least four areas in which pastors will have to engage to lead their churches into relevance: preaching, teaching, modeling, and balancing.

First, their preaching has to be oriented to help the church become a welcoming church. Intentional preaching about our mission to make Christlike disciples who in turn make Christlike disciples needs to be a priority. Preaching about the church as a welcoming place for all who are seek, journey, and even wander should also be intentional. This will result in a missional church, a going church, a welcoming church.

The second area of engagement is intentional teaching. We have already said this, but we need to emphasize it again. The teaching component of our discipleship efforts needs to make it intentional for all disciples (believers and seekers alike) to enter the Way, explore the Truth, and encounter the Life. As they refocus the teaching function in the church, pastors will need to lead their churches by training everyone into a discipleship lifestyle—whole-life discipleship.

Third, pastors need to model that lifestyle of discipleship as a journey of grace. Their pastoral practices need to be refocused to fit into the new paradigm. Practicing whole-life discipleship will allow pastors to become mentors themselves, finding cohorts of leaders within the church who in turn will practice and mentor others in the same disciplines. It is not enough to teach the new paradigm. The church needs to see the pastor and leaders as faithful imitators of the practices and lifestyle of the first-century church.

Finally, pastors need to balance the realities of an organic church that may be part of a larger family. In this balancing act, pastors need to have a clear understanding of the difference between institutional metrics and missional metrics. While these do not need to be mutually exclusive, the realities of being part of organizations with agreed-upon doctrines, covenants, and disciplines require the pastor to discern with clarity the organizational needs of both the missional and the institutional church. For example, many of our institutions use membership as a measurement of ministry success. This should be acceptable and enforced as needed for the ecclesial and polity requirements of each congregational and denominational definition. We should not throw away the ecclesiological importance of membership—but we need to understand that membership alone is not the most important metric of missional effectiveness. Membership is an important metric of ecclesial and organizational development.

At the same time, although membership has been historically one of the indicators of believers becoming part of a community they identify themselves with, pastors need to understand that, in a missional church, perhaps not everyone will become a member, even though they may enjoy and embrace the fellowship of the local congregation, the preaching, the doctrine, etc. This shouldn't be seen as a failure on the part of a pastor who has led the believers through the journey of grace. The pastor needs to manage that balance between believers becoming members of the community and becoming disciples of Jesus Christ. At the end of the day, Christlikeness is the work of the Holy Spirit in the life of the believer, while membership is the individual choice of the believer in covenant with the organized expression of the church they choose to join.

† Jerry

You know, we didn't keep a record of Sunday morning attendance until 1976. Before that, the only statistics we emphasized were Sunday school and membership. Sunday school attendance was usually greater than worship. A pastor needed to facilitate leadership development to be successful. At that time, the metric that measured church health and success was a growing Sunday school. But in the '70s we began to measure success differently. Along with the rest of culture we made the gold standard for success how many people were there for worship. It could be argued that we de-emphasized discipleship development when we made this change—by putting the emphasis on one person's message and the music that surrounded it. The production of the Sunday morning service became the focus. I may be overstating the case a bit, but the unintended consequence was a shift from leadership development to a focus on the sermon as the primary means of making disciples. I think a return to our roots on the issue of what we measure may be helpful. A good question to ask is, "How many disciples are being mentored and developed?" I think a change of emphasis could help.

§ Gustavo

Wouldn't it be, then, Jerry, that, by doing that, we created a misunderstanding of what welcoming means? Because one may say, "Hey, listen, we're measuring how many people are in our service because our services are where people realize we have a welcoming church because everybody's welcome to our Sunday service!" Perhaps that's one of the reasons we developed slogans like "our church can be your home" without developing the welcoming environment for everyone to feel at home in the church.

† Jerry

Recently I started asking the pastors under my leadership to focus their annual reports on a story about someone they were helping develop as a leader—someone they were excited about who can be a leader for the future of the church. Our impact in the community is enhanced when more voices are empowered to speak. People—and their stories of transformation and growth—are our greatest assets. When people are empowered to speak and lead, good things happen. Our resource allocation should reflect this leadership development priority.

∫ Stephanie

What I've been thinking about is not only how we steward our resources but also how we steward our time. So much of our time is devoted to, as has been said, the production on Sunday—the product we're trying to create. What would it look like for a pastor to be deeply engaged in the community in other meaningful ways? What if they had a relationship with the mayor or other civic leaders, the chamber of commerce, school principals, etc.? These are the kinds of relationships the pastor can cultivate so they become aware of the needs and concerns of the community. In knowing needs, we can better cooperate and bless our communities in meaningful ways. A pastor can model this type of engagement.

But it is also important for pastors to be students of culture as well. What are the pressing issues of our time? What are the questions people are asking, and where does the gospel intersect with those things? I'm not talking about rewriting sermons every Saturday night because something happened in the news. That's a dangerous place to live, and we must trust that the gospel is going to speak to those things through regular and faithful engagement with the biblical text. But what does it look like to pay attention to what's happening and to continually ask the Spirit to guide us in teaching and preaching in such a way that intersects with those questions and those struggles? We don't want to speak *past* people but *to* them in their need and their pain or place of confusion, doubt, and fear.

How can we intersect in those ways? How can we guide people to an alternative narrative, a story that is rooted in God's saving action and redemptive purposes instead of merely offering self-help tips? People don't need advice; they need a story that offers meaning to their lives and makes sense of the chaos around them. We have that story and can invite people to enter into it.

AFTERWORD
Gustavo Crocker

When we embarked on this writing project, we were not prepared for the exciting journey of mutual learning, accountability, and agreement. Writing this book has proved to be a good practice of what doing church today is all about. We didn't compromise the core, we didn't lose focus on the mission, yet we were open to make our thoughts and biases vulnerable for the sake of the church that we love and for whom Christ died.

The reader may, at times, have felt as if there were disjointed pieces in the flow of the book. That was intentional. We did it to prove that even a project of this nature needs to model what we want to happen in the church. Everyone's views are welcomed, tested, challenged, and affirmed with a spirit of love and honesty. We used the filter of both love and truth as a way to test the validity of our thoughts before they became part of this book. Our hope was and still is that this should also be the filter of the church as we surrender ourselves to the leading of the Holy Spirit to reorient our actions, our programs, and our witness.

"The Word became flesh and made his dwelling among us. We have seen his glory, the glory of the one and only Son, who came from the Father, full of grace and truth" (John 1:14). This is our prayer—that the church will be able to incarnate itself into the communities of the world and make a dwelling among them; that we will be able to display Christ, full of grace (love) and truth (light). Blessings.